Teachers Wanted

Attracting and Retaining Good Teachers

Daniel A. Heller

Association for Supervision and Curriculum Development
Alexandria, Virginia USA

Association for Supervision and Curriculum Development
1703 N. Beauregard St. • Alexandria, VA 22311-1714 USA
Telephone: 800-933-2723 or 703-578-9600 • Fax: 703-575-5400
Web site: http://www.ascd.org • E-mail: member@ascd.org

Gene R. Carter, *Executive Director;* Nancy Modrak, *Director of Publishing;*
Julie Houtz, *Director of Book Editing & Production;* Deborah Siegel, *Project
Manager;* Shelley Young, *Senior Graphic Designer;* BMWW, *Typesetter;*
Vivian Coss, *Production Specialist*

ASCD Member Book, No. FY04-8 (July 2004, PC). ASCD Member Books mail
to Premium (P), Comprehensive (C), and Regular (R) members on this
schedule: Jan., PC; Feb., P; Apr., PCR; May, P; July, PC; Aug., P; Sept., PCR;
Nov., PC; Dec., P.

Paperback ISBN: 0-87120-881-4 • ASCD product #104005 • List Price: $21.95
($16.95 ASCD member price, direct from ASCD only)
e-books ($21.95): netLibrary ISBN 1-4166-0051-5 • ebrary ISBN 1-4166-0052-3

Library of Congress Cataloging-in-Publication Data

Heller, Daniel A., 1953–
    Teachers wanted : attracting and retaining good teachers / Daniel A. Heller.
        p. cm.
    Includes bibliographical references (p.   ) and index.
    ISBN 0-87120-881-4 (alk. paper)
    1. Teachers—Recruiting—United States.   2. Teacher turnover—United
States—Prevention.   3. Teachers—Training of—United States.   I. Title.

    LB2835.25.H45 2004
    371.1—dc22   2004006156

10 09 08 07 06 05 04 03   12 11 10 9 8 7 6 5 4 3 2 1

To Nina and Ben, who have taught me
the most important lesson of all: how to love

Teachers Wanted
Attracting and Retaining Good Teachers

Acknowledgments

There are several individuals whom I must thank. First, Scott Willis has been a remarkable editor. His criticism was always insightful and gentle, while his encouragement and faith were continuous throughout the project. Another editor, Donovan R. Walling of Phi Delta Kappa International, was the first to read my proposed outline. He made several comments on my ideas and urged me to continue with the project. Jurg Jenzer always believed in me more than I did in myself, and he was not hesitant to let me know how he felt. Many long conversations with my colleague Deb Squires were clarifying and confirming with respect to the ideas I was developing in the book.

Of course, countless people have taught me many things along the way. I cannot forget my wife Nina and son Ben, the bedrocks of my life, whose belief in me never waivers, and who give me strength. Nina was a great help with the references, as well.

Finally, my appreciation goes to Stanley, who, no matter what time of day or night, whether my mood was one of joy, frustration, anger, or exhaustion, was always there to look up at me with those soft brown eyes, wagging his tail.

1

The Problem Defined

The fear of a teacher shortage, which is predicted to get worse over the next several years, pervades the profession. However, it is no longer a fear of something looming on the horizon; it is a reality. "Nationally, 60 percent of current teachers are eligible to retire in the next six years" (Brighton, 1999, p. 197). One need only place an advertisement to see how small the pools of viable candidates have become. Ten years ago, a single, small ad in the *Boston Globe* would bring me as many as 100 résumés, some from as far away as Japan. I was working in Vermont at the time, noted for its rural nature and poor salaries. More recently, working in Connecticut, noted for just the opposite conditions and in fact offering teachers some of the highest salaries in the nation, I could barely put together a pool of two or three candidates for a teaching position. At times, openings remained unfilled for months.

> [T]the current teacher shortage represents arguably the most imminent threat to the nation's schools. The U.S. Department of Education estimates that approximately 2.2 million teachers will be needed over the next decade—an average of more than 200,000 new teachers annually. (Howard, 2003, p. 1)

As recently as May 26, 2003, the *Miami Herald* reported that Florida would need at least 20,000–22,500 new teachers for the coming

1

fall, or an increase of 15 percent in the teaching force. Furthermore, the need for teachers is expected to grow over the next five years as large numbers of current teachers choose to take advantage of early retirement incentives (DeValle & de Vise, 2003, pp. 1–2).

What is happening within our profession, and what are we educational leaders going to do about it? If we do not take charge of the situation now, it will take charge of us.

Clearly, my experiences have uncovered diminishing numbers of young people entering the profession. At the same time, we know that we are in the midst of a large bulge of retiring teachers. Although it will be difficult to replace these retirees, we should also consider the wealth of knowledge and experience that will exit with them. The problem is larger than a shortage of warm bodies. It extends to the need to rebuild the base of knowledge about teaching, learning, and students held by veteran teaching staffs, which can be decimated by the loss of core, experienced teachers. Starting from scratch, or almost from scratch, is a daunting proposition.

At the same time, states are making entry into the profession ever more difficult.

> The challenge of attracting and retaining quality teachers is heightened by increased pressure for district and school accountability, often in the form of high-stakes testing and mandated curricular standards. In response to these mandates, districts are introducing reforms and initiatives at a frenetic pace. As a result, new teachers are struggling to learn their craft in dynamic and frequently chaotic environments. (Johnson, Birkeland, Kardos, Kauffman, & Peske, 2001, p. 6)

Again, I refer to my own experience. Having taught for 24 years, holding regular teaching licenses in secondary English and administration from both Vermont and New York, having earned advanced degrees in educational curriculum and instruction, English literature, and educational administration, and having been an administrator for 10 years, I found myself faced with a battery of requirements before I could obtain licenses in other states. After taking the Massachusetts Teacher Literacy test, all three Praxis I tests, and both Praxis II tests for English teachers, writing literally hundreds of pages describing my various experiences as an educator, and spending more than $1,000, I managed to extend my ability to teach or be an administrator to three more states. Certainly, the time and expense of acquiring the necessary credentials can be discouraging to young people just beginning a career in education. Recently, Illinois introduced state legislation to require "aspiring teachers to pass a basic-skills test before entering colleges' teacher education programs, a standard that could set one of the earliest such deadlines in the country" (Cavanaugh, 2002, p. 20).

My point here is that while the number of teachers is decreasing, we are at the same time making entry into the profession more difficult. Obviously, raising the bar makes sense. We want the education of our children in the hands of the most competent, knowledgeable teachers possible. However, the timing of these efforts is problematic, and I fear that, in an effort to improve the quality of the teaching force, we may actually be maneuvering ourselves into a position where we will have to issue numerous emergency licenses to fill the many vacancies, thus effectively weakening, not strengthening, America's cadre of teachers. This problem existed even before the initiation of the new, more rigorous licensing requirements, especially in areas where schools have been experiencing difficulties in attracting well-qualified teachers.

> Some responses to the teacher shortage, however, contradict the mounting evidence that teacher preparation matters. Administrators, especially those in the largest urban areas, routinely hire individuals with no preparation. They do not want to do this, but the conditions in some schools make it difficult to attract and retain qualified teachers. (Wise, 2003, p. 43)

Issuing temporary or emergency licenses will not help in the long run, and in the short run they will serve only to put unqualified adults in front of classes that would otherwise have no teachers at all.

> Alternative certification (including temporary and emergency certification) and alternatives to certification (let anyone teach) will not do the job. In a misleading use of language, these certificates literally mean that

the state is certifying that these certificate holders are not yet certifiable under the state's own laws and regulations. Dissembling is not a strategy for enhancing public confidence. (Wise, 2003, p. 43)

In one particular Vermont school district, the situation for 2001–2002 looked like this: Out of the total number of teachers in the district, 20 percent were new hires. Additionally, 20 percent of the district's teachers were in their first or second year of teaching. Finally, 19 percent of all district teachers were employed under waivers because they did not have full licensure. Several positions simply remained unfilled or were covered by principals, cutting into their time for working with other teachers and programs.

The new federal legislation, the No Child Left Behind Act, recognizes this issue at a national level by giving parents the right to know the qualifications of their children's teachers and paraprofessionals, and whether their children have been taught for four or more consecutive weeks by a teacher who is not considered highly qualified, which I take to mean holding the required state license or certificate for his or her particular teaching position.

Add to this the increasing demands placed on teachers. They must be counselors, reporting agents for the state in cases of abuse, disciplinarians, individuals skilled in making accommodations for students with learning disabilities, curriculum writers, club advisers, athletic coaches, and record keepers. I have seen everything from crisis deescalation training to alcohol and drug abuse training offered for educators. There seems to be no end to the duties required of teachers. Is this the career that a 22-year-old English major envisions when he or she contemplates the joys of sharing his or her passion with new students?

Attrition Rates

Teachers have one of the highest attrition rates of any profession; in particular, new teachers are apt to leave our schools. A study published in the *American Educational Research Journal* and conducted by Richard M. Ingersoll, an associate professor of education and sociology at Philadelphia University, corroborates this point. According to Ingersoll's findings, the average yearly turnover rate in education is 13.2 percent as compared to 11 percent in other professions. Even more significant to the problem under discussion here is that 29 percent of new teachers leave education within their first three years, and by the end of five years, 39 percent have left (Viadero, 2002, p. 7). Ingersoll concludes that educators should spend less time on recruitment efforts and put more effort into retaining the teachers they have.

> Schools might have better luck meeting their demands for teachers . . . by making improvements in job conditions, such as increasing support for teachers, raising salaries, reducing student misbehavior, and giving faculty members more say in school decision making. (Viadero, 2002, p. 7)

To make matters worse, the teachers who leave tend to be the best new recruits (Gordon & Maxey, 2000, p. 8).

We find ourselves in a catch-22 situation: We are desperate for people to enter a profession with standards that are increasingly difficult to meet, has ever-expanding duties, and can easily crush the idealism of a new member. Several questions arise as we contemplate the current circumstances. How do we prepare and attract more qualified people into the profession? How do we keep them in our schools? Education is notorious for low survival rate of new teachers, which prompted Halford to call education "the profession that eats its young" (Renard, 1999, p. 227). How can we either hold onto veteran teachers a little longer or at least capture their wisdom for the next generation of teachers?

The answers to these questions involve collaborative efforts among institutions of higher learning, state teacher licensing bodies, local communities, primary and secondary schools, teachers' associations, and, of course, educational administrators, who will have to reorient their priorities to address the complex changes needed. The principal stands at the nexus of change, and many of the responsibilities involved in solving the problems presented by the teacher shortage will fall to the principal.

New Teacher Training

In the typical teacher training program, students actually experience schools for the first time quite late in their education. How sad to spend two or three years studying pedagogy only to find out that teaching school is not what you thought it would be. Exposure to actual classrooms and teachers and schools and students should be an ongoing part of teacher preparation, from freshman year to graduation. This approach would allow students to drop out of education and change majors before it is too late. We need to rethink the entire process of teacher training—balancing rigor, support, and reality all along the way.

Teacher induction programs, led by veteran teachers, supported by colleges and universities, and held together by building and district administrators, will need to prepare high-quality teachers without being so discouraging as to turn promising candidates to other professions. Isolation is a primary reason that new teachers leave, and consequently about 30 states have invested in new teacher programs. The research has shown that when new teachers are left to their own devices, they tend to leave the profession (DeValle & de Vise, 2003, p. 3). Principals will have to spend more time than ever before in formative supervision roles, nurturing new teachers. "New teachers perceive building principals to be a vital link in their success" (Danin & Bacon, 1999, p. 206). If we find ourselves in the position of granting waivers and hiring willing teachers who have not had the requisite experience and training, then these induction programs will become of paramount importance. Schools will need to internalize programs designed to rapidly develop the necessary skills and knowledge, without sacrificing quality, of nontraditional first-year teachers as well as those of traditionally trained personnel.

In historical terms, the principal must once again become the lead or principal teacher, not the manager, of a building. Unless we rethink the whole concept of the principal's role as an educational leader, a teacher of teachers, then there is little hope of bringing into our schools the type of talent that we need. The principal will have the responsibility of creating an institutional atmosphere of collaboration and support, as opposed to one in which individual teachers shut their doors and operate privately. New teachers should not be left to learn wholly by experience, when the knowledge and support they need resides in the room next to theirs.

New Models for a New World

The old model of seniority in distributing teaching assignments is a major reason for new teacher attrition. It is no wonder that new teachers leave the profession when we routinely assign them (the most inexperienced members of the faculty) the most challenging classes (Feiman-Nemser, Carver, Schwille, & Yusko, 1999, p. 5). Shouldn't master teachers teach those tough classes, being the professionals with the highest level of skill? Would you go to someone just out of medical school for a delicate neurosurgical procedure? Mentors, supports, and scaffolding should be in place all along the way toward becoming a competent and consummate teacher. Such a structure would have the added benefit of providing a career ladder for teachers, supporting the concept of master teachers and teacher mentors. Often the only way to advance in the world of education currently is to leave the classroom and become an administrator. We should reward excellent teachers with more sophisticated teaching duties, such as becoming professional development directors or teachers of teachers, as well as with higher salaries. Why do we think that the skills that make an excellent teacher are the same skills needed to be an excellent administrator? Administration is by no means simply an expansion of teaching.

Old Knowledge and New Knowledge

How can we recoup the knowledge and experience of the veteran teachers? How can we induce them to stay a while longer to give a hand up to the next generation? Once more, administrators will play a critical role in developing and implementing programs dedicated to creating a role for these people. At best, qualified veterans should be paid as master teachers to work with new staff, and at the very least, we should staff inservice programs with retired teachers hired to share their expertise, teach courses, and mentor their replacements. Teaching can be lonely, especially for the first-year teacher. There is so much to do, in addition to adapting to the culture of the school. A critical friend could provide just the lifeline needed to keep a good teacher going or to help counsel a poor teacher out of the profession. In fact, mentors have been shown to increase teacher retention (Kelly, 2001, p. 5).

Education has often been referred to as an art. To some extent, this description is true. Not all people are cut out to be teachers; not everyone has the temperament. Much of what a teacher does depends on his or her ability to establish relationships with young people, to make rapid decisions, to flow with the process of teaching and learning. However, the last two decades have produced a wealth of knowledge about brain function, cognitive processes, multiple intelligences, the importance of emotional stability, effective discipline interventions, and numerous alternatives to the traditional methods of education. Education today entails at least as much science as art. Proper training in cognitive psychology and brain-based learning is an absolute necessity. Here, we need a balance of rigor and support for those entering the profession.

Throwing well-meaning people who like kids at the vacancies is not the answer. Blindly raising licensing standards without the necessary supports is not the answer. A sink-or-swim mentality for the treatment of new teachers is just plain wrong. We wouldn't allow teachers to treat their own students that way, so why should we treat professionals in this manner? Allowing the veterans to leave with all their knowledge and wisdom is short-sighted. The problems of the teacher shortage are many; the solutions complex, difficult, and nontraditional.

New Roles for Principals

In the middle of all this is the principal, whose job must rapidly become liquid in its ability to change and adapt to what is happening. The principal stands at the crossroads of the faculty, students, parents, community, board, state policymakers, and representatives of higher education. Creativity and the freedom to use it will be key. Principals must be empowered to make decisions, take risks, and try new approaches. Trust will be a crucial component of the changes to come. Not only must school boards and parents be involved with their children's education, but they also must be willing to allow educational leaders the latitude to do what has to be done. Changes can take time. They can be messy. We will all have to increase our tolerance for ambiguity and uncertainty. Management activities will have to give way to educational leadership, leaving others to take care of daily operations. Principals will be responsible for breathing new life into the system, negotiating complex changes, convincing the community and state powers of the need to change and of the changes needed. Perhaps "chief of educational staff" is a more appropriate name for this new leader than the former title of principal. Hospitals may serve as a model that separates managing the institution from performing the functions of the institution. The chief of staff is not the CEO of the hospital's administration. Millie Pierce, the director of the Principals' Center at the Harvard Graduate School of Education, makes this suggestion about the principal's job:

> [P]erhaps two leaders are needed in every school: a principal teacher and a principal administrator. The principal teacher would have a well-established teaching history rooted in strong instructional practice. This person would spend the year supervising teaching teams, coaching, giving feedback, and teaching teachers to engage in deep, reflective practice on unambiguous learning outcomes. The principal teacher would be accountable for student achievement, curriculum, and technology, and have authority to hire and fire.
>
> Meanwhile, the principal administrator's position would focus on plant management. (Pierce, 2000, p. 7)

New Opportunities

The teacher shortage need not be seen as a terrible problem. Rather, it may be the greatest opportunity presented to the educational system of the United States in a century. Imagine a whole cadre of new teachers, without emotional baggage, without expectations of the way things have always been done, without the cynicism so often found within school faculties. The way to change a school is through the hiring process. Certainly, finding people with the right qualifications and attitude is easier than trying to change people already established and comfortable in their roles. If all the pieces come together, the opportunity to hire a large number of teachers is also an opportunity to shape a school. Astute principals will hire new teachers who have the particular qualities and philosophies that they want. In this way, educational leaders will be able to create a critical mass of like-minded people, ready to take on the challenges that lie ahead in teaching. Rather than fighting resistance to change, principals may recognize the need to hire a large number of teachers as an opportunity to innovate without having to ask people to leave their long-standing comfort zones.

The Purpose of This Book

The purpose of this book is to suggest several models in response to the areas of need mentioned earlier: preservice, induction, inservice, and retention. Principals will have to lead the necessary changes to make their schools attractive workplaces for new teachers, with climates that attract applicants and encourage employees to stay, satisfying their professional needs. This strategy means that school philosophies, missions, and visions should define workplaces that provide for those professional needs. Gardner, Csikszentmihalyi, and Damon (2001), in their book *Good Work*, clearly articulate the problem of attracting and retaining new people to a profession:

> [H]armonious professional realms exist when individual practitioners are attracted to the domains that most suit their interests and abilities, when they are allowed to develop and grow within the parameters of the practice, and when their rewards are commensurate with their skills and contributions. If a profession cannot offer the opportunity for doing good work—in the sense of providing flow experiences and enabling individuals to do their best in meaningful occupations—young people unsuited by talent or temperament will enter whatever field pays better or gives the most prestige. (p. 30)

In each stage of teacher development, the principal will have a crucial role to play. Creativity, leadership style, communication, diplomacy, and knowledge are all significant pieces of the process. I will explore these models, sources of revenue, and the principal's role in the educational reform spurred by the teacher shortage. At first blush, the task appears daunting. It is. But it is doable, and perhaps the most exciting possibility for educational reform in generations.

The current weakened state of the economy has caused many state and local education budgets to shrink, resulting in teacher lay-offs. However, when the economy rebounds, we will find ourselves still searching for a full cadre of highly qualified teachers. Further-more, the fact that the economy is forcing people to stay in their jobs does not address the conditions of education that, in better times, can—and, as I will argue, do—drive good teachers away. Those conditions have an effect on morale, teacher quality, and teaching as a profession, and they may result in an atmosphere that does not support teachers in doing their best work. This situation ultimately affects teaching and learning—the experience of the student. Regardless of the political or economic situation, we have to take a long, critical look at the conditions under which we train teachers, ask them to work and remain in the field, and expect them to see themselves as true professionals. The following chapters are an attempt to do just that.

Preservice Education

A way to avoid the competition for an inadequate supply of new and well-trained personnel is to establish partnerships between primary and secondary schools and training institutions, thus introducing new and emerging teachers directly to a principal's school. In fact, a principal might see his or her school as a "teaching school" or "professional development school" in the same way that certain hospitals are "teaching hospitals," known for the superior training they provide for interns. The process begins with making contact with the teacher preparation program.

Public School and Higher Education Partnerships

Contact with teacher preparation programs will hopefully lead to an actual negotiation between the college and the school around issues of training exchanges and establishing schools and higher education as equal partners in the process of preparing the next generation of teachers. For instance, if the school can offer a particularly fine student teaching experience for college students, then perhaps the college will not only regard the school as a primary training institution but also offer services, such as specific courses, study groups to address issues at the school, and even teacher–professor exchange programs in exchange for this superior intern training. The more improvement the university can bring to the school, the better training ground it has prepared for its own student interns.

12

Recently, the Carnegie Corporation of New York launched an initiative to improve teacher education programs that is very much in line with these ideas. Participating schools of education will be required to make several changes in their programs.

> Those include increasing involvement in teacher training of both practicing K–12 teachers and faculty members from the arts and sciences, giving teacher-candidates more experience in the classroom, and monitoring graduates once on the job to see how well their students perform. . . . Participants are expected to make several major changes meant to give teacher-candidates better preparation in both subject matter and in the practicalities of working in the classroom. (Archer, 2002, p. 5)

I remember one such relationship that led to all of the social studies interns at the local college substituting for every member of the social studies department of the local high school, thus allowing the social studies teachers to go on a much-needed retreat to discuss pressing educational concerns. In fact, the college even provided a space for the teachers to work in exchange for the real experience their interns received teaching in those classrooms. The interns had done significant and specific preparation ahead of time so they were familiar with the material they would be teaching.

Benefits for Public School and Higher Education

Let's imagine what a good working relationship between a college and a local school or school system might look like. To begin with, students interested in the teaching profession would get their feet wet early, in their freshman year. Their first contact would be in the role of observer and, at times, paraprofessional in the school. In this way, the intern could see what a real school looks and feels like in operation, rather than simply reading about teaching and learning. Two reasons that novice teachers leave the profession are the disparity between their preparation and the actual requirements of the job, and the disparity between the new teacher's expectations and the realities of the job (Brighton, 1999, pp. 198–199). At the same time, key members of the school community—teachers, principals, supervisors, and students—would become familiar with the prospective intern. This approach would test the mettle of the intern who then might decide that teaching was the wrong choice. He or she would still have time to change direction, as opposed to the current situation, in which interns usually have little real experience with schools and teaching until their senior year. This long-term relationship would also alert the hosting school to any potential problems. Either party would have the option to terminate the relationship at any time, but the typical course of events would have the teaching intern involved at various levels within the school for four years.

Teachers College and New York City Public Schools

In 1988, Teachers College of Columbia University and two New York City public schools began to discuss developing a collaboration not unlike the one described here for the purposes of improving the relationship between higher education and public education, and creating an improved system of teacher preparation. Their idea of a professional development school involved bringing the research knowledge of the university together with the practical knowledge of the teachers from one elementary school and one intermediate school. The program centered around a two-year master's program in education. All degree candidates in the program student-taught for two semesters (in the past, secondary content specialist teachers had only student-taught for one semester) during the first year, as well as continuing academic course work. Public school teachers took on a good deal of the student-teacher seminar design and teaching, as opposed to staff from the university. The student-teaching experience involved working with two different teachers at two different grade levels. Cooperating teachers had to take a course on supervision from the university, which was cotaught by university personnel and public school teachers.

By the end of the first year, the students were eligible for certification. At this point, they became teacher-interns in their respective schools. At the elementary level, the intern worked with two teachers on a team that dealt with two classes of students in various configurations. The intermediate-level interns worked in a variety of classes while having one teacher-mentor. Toward the end of the second year, teacher-interns took over their classes completely for six weeks, freeing the master teachers to pursue individually designed professional development activities. Public school teachers organized and ran credit-bearing seminars for the teacher interns. In the third year, the interns became actual teachers but continued being mentored by the teachers they had worked with during their intern year (Snyder, 1994, p. 99).

Key elements of this program included

• More extended time in classrooms with intense supervision and guided reflection;

• Opportunities to observe and work with more than one group of students;

• Opportunities to observe and work with more than one approach to teaching;

• Team teaching;

• Professional collaboration; and

• Improved linkages between college and school experiences (Snyder, 1994, p. 100).

Other examples of effective partnerships between public schools and postsecondary teacher preparation programs can be found in Wells, Maine (Miller & Silvernail, 1994, pp. 28–49), and the Puget Sound Professional Development Center (Grossman, 1994, pp. 50–73).

Creating a Learning Community

For a partnership to develop between a school and a teacher preparation program, the principal needs to establish a certain climate. To be part of a professional development institution, teachers must be in the mode of always growing and learning themselves. This love of teaching and learning would pervade the entire atmosphere of the school. Asked about her experiences as a new teacher, a Vermont English teacher responded, "It may help to remember that, not only did you [the supervisor] interview and hire new teachers, they [the prospective teachers] interviewed you to see if you would provide an environment conducive to personal and professional growth" (Harvey, Heller, McConnell, & Williams, 1998, p. 139).

Principals can support this professional atmosphere in several ways. First, they have to model being constant learners themselves. If the principal does not set the example and expectation that everyone will engage in meaningful professional development at all times, then who will? Next, the principal should be in classrooms frequently, on both a formal and an informal basis, observing teachers and working with them to improve their skills. In fact, the principal should be capable of delivering and leading professional development sessions for the staff rather than always relying on outside resources for this purpose.

To further develop this climate of continuous professional development, the principal will have to empower teachers as professional developers themselves. At any given time, a percentage of teachers are taking courses, attending workshops, attending conferences, or reading professional literature. Why not make a habit of asking teachers to lead inservice programs for each other, thus honoring them as professionals and saving the expense of costly outside consultants? Even paying a teacher his or her per diem would be less expensive than the price of outside people. For this to happen, the principal will have to encourage teachers to attend professional development activities and then require that the teachers at least write a report of what they have learned. Then if there is sufficient interest, the experience could lead to a full-blown inservice program. A common characteristic of the professional development schools described earlier was the use of master classroom teachers as instructors for new teacher seminars.

The Power of Teachers Talking to Teachers

While employed as a central administrator in southern Vermont, I surveyed a school district to determine teachers' interests for inservice activities. I then produced another survey to find out what teachers were willing to present. Matching these two collections of data, the District Inservice Committee and I developed a series of 10 after-school, one-hour presentations and 5 after-school, one-hour book conversations. Teachers and administrators from the district delivered all but one of the presentations. The sessions were well attended, and evaluation forms were generally positive. Topics included Brain Gym, Phonemic Awareness, Brain-Based Teaching, Constructivism, Learning Styles, Taking Kids Outside—Teaching Sensory Activities, Teaching Narrative, Burnout, Teaching Technology, and Using Multiple Intelligences to Learn the Continents and Oceans. Each presenter earned $100, and we provided refreshments at each session. Since this series of inservice activities, Brain Gym (a method of using body movement to stimulate the brain for learning) has become very popular, with individual principals arranging several more training sessions. Requests have been made for repeats of the sessions on brain-based learning and constructivism and also for advanced-level sessions on these topics for those who attended last year. Finally, four teachers later approached me about support for new inservice workshops for interested members of the district. Teachers were seeing themselves as professionals, the district was gaining excellent inservice programs, and the cost was minimal.

According to Regie Routman (2002), a writer on educational issues, "knowledgeable, well-informed teachers make a greater difference than do specific programs" (p. 32). She sees conversation as a very powerful professional development tool that should be built into the school day. In other words, the best people to teach teachers are other teachers. I will explore this concept in greater detail later, when I discuss the use of peer supervision as a major component of creating an atmosphere of professional growth in a school.

Briefly, the principal can help teachers find ways of observing one another. The basic idea is that teachers are perfectly capable of teaching each other. If I am teaching *Hamlet* for the first time, who better to assist me than my colleague across the hall who has taught the work several times? The more opportunities teachers have to control their own professional development practices, the more the climate will develop into one of continual teacher learning. In fact, the goal is to create a learning community engaged in ongoing professional development. At that point, having an observer in a classroom will become such a common occurrence that students will virtually ignore the adult in the back of the room. I know this from experience.

The Cost of Innovation

Obviously, this kind of continuous professional development does come with a price, but it is surprisingly inexpensive and certainly less expensive than some of the more traditional delivery systems for teacher education. The currency here is time. Teachers must have time to observe one another's classes, time to reflect, time to prepare presentations. The principal plays a central role here. He or she has to be willing to take over classes to release teachers to make observations. Another resource could be hiring roving substitutes from time to time who could release various teachers throughout the day. In fact, one or two paraprofessionals might be brought on board just for this purpose. Lastly, the principal can support this concept with budget proposals, and be willing to fight for them. The principal is the primary connection between the school and the school board. Therefore, it becomes incumbent on him or her to help boards understand the advantages of this approach to professional development, not only for the satisfaction of current teachers but for the attraction and retention of new teachers in the future.

Where will the money come from? Let's begin with whatever is already allocated for professional development. The principal will have to spend this money differently than in the past, to fund the ideas presented here. Imagine if money spent on recruitment were reallocated to training and ongoing professional development.

> Recruiters in various districts can now waive training, offer signing bonuses, forgive student loans, and even provide mortgage subsidies or health club memberships. While such strategies may well increase the supply of new teachers to schools, they provide no assurance of keeping them there, for they are but short-term responses to long-term challenges. (Johnson et al., 2001, p. 8)

Also, we should keep in mind that this book is about the teacher shortage. Large-scale retirement and new hiring means substantial savings in salaries. By shifting costs from salary lines to professional development lines, one could potentially keep the budget to a minimal increase or no increase at all, while at the same time releasing money for professional development. Theoretically, as the new teachers rise on the salary scale, the money could move back to the salary line. By that time, those new teachers would be experienced teachers, and the extraordinary expenses of training and induction should have tapered down. I will discuss all of these ideas at greater length later in this book, particularly in the chapter on inservice programs.

One other important advantage to this model of inservice education is its practical value. Rather than paying an outside expert to present information to a large group, here we have teachers working intimately with one another. The necessary follow-up and coaching, which have been shown to be so important in professional development, can take place. In other words, the school will get more for its money if it makes use of the internal resources already within the system and allows increased opportunities for teachers to engage in the professional roles of training and gatekeeping, which have traditionally been withheld from them.

Gatekeeping

The authors of *Good Work* (Gardner et al., 2001) address the concept of a profession's gatekeepers in this way:

> Individual practitioners in a field occupy one of three major roles. The elite are the *gatekeepers* who preside over the destiny of the professional realm and judge which changes in the domain should be sanctioned. Some fields recognize a hierarchy of gatekeepers, whereas others do not. Gatekeepers emerge as a result of complex interactions among practitioners that involve politics, reputation, respect, and appointment to key institutional positions. In medicine the ranks of gatekeepers include the medical directors of major funding institutions such as the National Institutes of Health (NIH), the deans and department heads of major medical schools, the editors of respected medical journals such as *The New England Journal of Medicine* and *The Lancet,* and so on. (p. 25)

In education, the gatekeepers traditionally have been state licensing agencies and postsecondary preparation programs. A necessary step in the process of changing the profession would be to expand the gatekeeping role to include practicing teachers and administrators. Adam Urbanski, the president of the Rochester Teachers Association, says that "taking the responsibility for who qualifies to become a teacher and who deserves to remain a teacher is the job, first and foremost, of teachers themselves" (Kelly, 2001, p. 6).

If a principal could offer this type of an atmosphere—a real "professional development school" devoted to teacher growth—to a college or university as a training lab for interns, then I believe that there would be little reason for the institution of higher learning to object and every reason to cultivate the relationship. As Levine (2002) describes the possible scenario:

> School faculty members bring their knowledge of practice to the partnership; university faculty members bring their research knowledge and inquiry skills. . . . Professional development schools bring strong candidates into schools to collaborate with experienced mentor teachers on instructional teams. Candidates do not have full teaching responsibility, and they and their mentors have time to address the candidates' needs. (p. 65)

I am not naive. School–university partnerships do not just happen. Issues of ego and territory abound. Eventually, though, those partnerships that have been successful have moved beyond these issues to the common goal of producing excellent new teachers.

Continuing with my proposal of a four-year intern–school relationship (in which the first year would be spent in the role of observer and, at times, paraprofessional), in the intern's second year, he or she could function as a tutor or monitor; in the third year, as a teaching assistant; and in the fourth year, as an actual intern. Imagine how much richer the experience would be for the intern, and think of the increased likelihood that the intern would stay on as a regular staff member. Moreover, the principal and staff would have had four years of observing this candidate before making the decision to offer a position. By the same token, the prospective new teacher would have gained sufficient knowledge of the school to know whether it would be a good match in style and philosophy. In addition, with interns in the building for four years, that many additional hands would be available to cover the many tasks involved in operating a school: record keeping, photocopying, supervising the playground, grading papers, developing curriculum, and coaching.

We are discussing the teacher shortage, and one of the reasons for it, as we have seen, is the extraordinary attrition rate of new teachers. However, "the attrition rate of the professional development school graduates was one-third that of graduates of traditional programs," according to a consultant for the National Council for Accreditation of Teacher Education (NCATE) (Levine, 2002, p. 67). As another example:

> Before implementing the [induction] program in 1996, Lafourche Parish [in Louisiana] had a 51 percent annual teacher attrition rate. That rate decreased to 15 percent almost immediately upon implementation of the program. Today, the district's teacher attrition hovers around 7 percent—a decrease of approximately 80 percent since the inception of the induction program. (Wong, 2002, p. 54)

If we go one step further and consider induction programs growing out of preservice programs in professional development schools, we will have even more success at holding on to well-trained teachers.

Clearly, investing wisely in teacher preparation and induction pays off in developing better teachers who are more likely to remain in the profession, while also offering the side benefits of enhancing professional development opportunities and professional esteem (as gatekeepers of the profession) for all teachers.

Training and Benefits for Experienced Teachers

School–university partnerships would require the college to provide training and compensation for cooperating teachers. Great teachers do not automatically make great teachers of teachers without some help. Knowing how to observe instruction, communicate one's observations, and then help the intern progress from there is not a simple task. Some instruction in adult learning will be necessary. "The same methods a teacher uses successfully to teach children may not work when the teacher is trying to promote the growth of beginning teachers" (Gordon & Maxey, 2000, p. 40). Instruction in classroom observation and conference techniques would be provided by the college, because training cooperating teachers is in its own best interest. This approach has the further advantage of enhancing teachers' ability to observe one another effectively and to analyze their own teaching.

The training and materials developed by Research for Better Teaching in Acton, Massachusetts, are particularly effective for this purpose. Teachers should receive at least continuing education units (CEUs) for this course work, if not actual graduate credit. This kind of attention honors experienced teachers, effectively making them master teachers. They should expect some compensation from the university for their time and efforts. Another example is noteworthy:

> In professional development partnerships with the University of Colorado (Denver), school faculty members can become Teachers in Residence at the university. They coteach courses, help supervise teacher candidates, and pursue their own professional development. . . . Professional development school partners can provide rewards and incentives for candidates and faculty members who take on new roles, and these institutions should reorganize to support new roles and new work. (Levine, 2002, p. 67)

A monthly seminar can provide needed support for cooperating teachers during the teacher-intern training process. This seminar would be a time to allow these teachers to share their experiences and to help out one another with any particular issues that have arisen. They could share coaching techniques, for example. Perhaps a teacher is looking for a kind way to share an observation with an intern that documents a particularly poor performance. Another teacher may be working with an intern who is having trouble with a few students acting out; other teachers could make suggestions for how to coach the intern. The seminar would break the loneliness that is so typical of the teaching profession and also serve as a decompression mechanism, allowing teachers to speak freely with one another and perhaps develop improvements in the intern program.

According to Routman (2002), teacher group conversations enhance student learning. She refers to one teacher who expressed the result of incorporating regular teacher conversation into the school program this way: "There is a unity of teachers in our building that wasn't there before. We are open to new ideas and always looking for a good 'professional read.' We have grown professionally as a staff" (p. 34). According to Moffett (2000), "more than almost any other factor, the sense of a professional community in schools enhances student achievement" (p. 36). If we see the student interns as these master teachers' students, then the idea of weekly meetings to discuss the program makes pedagogical, professional, and personal sense.

Student Intern Seminar

A similar seminar could exist for the interns themselves. They, too, need to process their experiences with peers. This sharing is especially effective when interns see that others are having the same problems and challenges that they are. They, too, can offer one another assistance and suggestions. This group should meet more often than the teacher group, as frequently as once each week. The group will also need a leader, a neutral party from the hosting school who could facilitate the discussion and help interns find the materials and resources to solve their problems. A particularly effective technique is for the interns to keep journals of their experiences. A day or two before each meeting, the facilitator collects the journals. Before the next meeting, he or she reads them and writes any comments that might be helpful. Then, the facilitator can choose something provocative from one of the journals to use as a starting point for the discussion at the next meeting.

A key feature of the intern group is, once again, to avoid the loneliness that so often accompanies student teaching. Just having others to share one's experiences with can release a great deal of tension and consequently ease the process. The sessions also provide an opportunity to vent. Frustrations, unhappiness with cooperating teachers or the college supervisor, disappointments with the program, and anger at disruptive students are all fair game for the discussion. Just like teachers, interns will need to learn how to deal with these feelings if they are to become successful professionals. Better to practice this difficult skill in a collaborative environment rather than alone in one's first professional position.

This design, then, is one more way to mitigate the potential trauma experienced in the transition from college student to intern to actual teacher. I have facilitated such a group of teaching interns, and I can honestly say that they appreciated the experience for all of the reasons cited here as well as for the personal attention they received. The seminar sent a message that the school cared about the welfare of these students.

Introducing Interns to the School Community

Because we are trying to give interns a complete training experience, we should introduce them to the entire school community and the various functions that it serves. Once each week, the interns could meet with a different person representing a specific aspect of the school. Here, too, the process honors the experienced teachers by calling on them to present to the group of interns.

The syllabus for this seminar needs to be comprehensive. What follows is a brief description of what some of the sessions might include:

• *Guidance:* A school counselor explains the purpose of and services provided by the school counseling office. The counselor would discuss topics such as mandatory reporting, confidentiality, and signs of trouble. The interns might discuss one or two brief case studies or present some of their own classroom observations for the group to examine.

• *Discipline:* A teacher, administrator, or dean of students would lead this session on basic classroom management and the discipline system in place at the school. What are the procedures one follows with a difficult child in this school? What forms need to be completed? Certainly, in addition to these procedural aspects of the discipline system, the group would examine basic techniques of classroom management, deescalation, and relationship building.

• *Administration:* This seminar would be the principal's opportunity to speak at length and directly with the interns. School philosophy, procedures, and resources would be useful topics here. What is the hiring process? What does the principal look for in a prospective teacher? How can the administration support teaching and learning in the building?

• *Academic area specialists:* These sessions might be devoted to the curriculum in various academic areas such as math, English, social studies, foreign language, and science. Interns, as well as teachers, should understand the whole school and how all the pieces fit together, rather than remaining in their isolated subject area or grade level.

• *Nurse:* The school nurse's role is a crucial area for interns to understand. It has grown tremendously in sophistication over the years, to the point where some nurse's offices are operating almost as small clinics. In a large school, the nurse may see upward of 100 students each day. Certainly, interns should know about this service, what nurses provide, and what they cannot.

• *Specialty areas:* Additional areas such as reading specialist assistance, tutoring programs, the library, and the computer lab can be presented and explained to interns as part of their experience at the school.

• *Special education:* Interns will need an introduction to the complexities of special education and various methods for meeting student accommodations.

New Structures for New Approaches

Interns need to be encouraged, if not required, to participate in all aspects of the school as any teacher would. They should sit with their cooperating teachers during parent conferences. They should participate in supervisory duties. Interns can be members of committees, and they can help coach athletics or advise clubs. As professionals, we have an obligation to nurture our profession, helping develop the next generation of teachers.

This description is designed to demonstrate what a symbiosis between a school and an institution of higher learning might look like. There is one more point to make, and a major one at that. A school–university partnership will require restructuring of roles, responsibilities, and schedules. In fact, the partnership may provide the necessary impetus to restructure. At any rate, as we contemplate doing business in new ways, old constructs will no longer necessarily support our work. Darling-Hammond (1994) describes this issue at one elementary professional development school in the Los Angeles School District:

> [T]eachers keenly feel the need to restructure the school schedule and create time for collaboration as they proceed with fundamental reforms. As they explore new models of teaching, develop units for thematic, interdisciplinary learning and link these with authentic assessment, initiate peer coaching and collegial planning, and launch problem-based clinics for teachers, the need to use school time differently has become apparent. (p. 17)

There are no easy answers to this problem, and I will not pretend to offer any. Each school must work through the issues of time and structure individually. However, throughout the book I will refer to what various schools have done in this regard. We have already seen several suggestions, including the principal covering classes for teachers, student interns covering classes, and using paraprofessionals or roving substitutes to release teachers for other duties.

The advantages of such a system accrue to both parties, with the major winners being the interns and the teaching profession. When you throw into the bargain having a direct line on newly prepared teachers, teachers whom you have prepared for your own school, you will also have taken a large step toward beating the challenge of the teacher shortage. You will be recapturing the experience of the senior staff as they work with the interns, and you will be molding the interns to fit your school's philosophy, vision, and mission. The climate you are creating is one that will support teacher retention rather than one that encourages teachers to leave for better situations (see Figure 2.1).

FIGURE 2.1

Advantages of School–University Partnerships for Teacher-Intern Training Programs

College	School	Teacher	Intern	Principal
• A fertile ground for training interns	• Training for teachers	• Training in observation of instruction and teacher techniques that could be applied within the staff	• Four years of school experience with a timely chance to decide that teaching is not the right profession	• A professional development school
• A complete training experience for work in public schools	• The beginnings of a teacher career ladder	• A chance to take on roles of responsibility, especially regarding the maintenance of the profession	• A complete training experience	• University resources
• Trained, interested, and professional cooperating teachers	• A means of capturing experienced teachers' knowledge	• Partnership in the elite function of gatekeeping	• An opportunity to work with trained cooperating teachers	• Teachers in professional roles of respect and gatekeeping
• Long-term experience for interns	• Extra hands on the job	• Career ladder structures	• A chance to work in many areas and with many aspects of the school	• An internal system of professional development, teacher to teacher
	• A long look at potential employees	• A chance to share with other cooperating teachers	• A chance to share with other student interns	• A climate conducive to having good teachers remain in teaching
• A direct link to well-trained new teachers for potential hire			• A chance to work directly into a professional position	

Induction Programs

Having established a key role in the preparation of new teachers, the principal must now develop induction programs to integrate new hires into the system to ensure that they have a successful experience and remain with the school. According to the Project on the Next Generation of Teachers at the Harvard Graduate School of Education:

> [O]ur research suggests that the key to addressing shortages lies not in active recruitment policies but in support and training for new teachers at the school site. For it is in schools and classrooms where teachers must find success and satisfaction. It is there they will decide whether or not to continue to teach. (Johnson et al., 2001, p. 8)

This point will be particularly crucial with respect to teachers who come to the profession through nontraditional routes and who may not have adequate background or training.

There may very well be times when a principal is forced to hire nontraditional or nonlicensed personnel. This situation in and of itself is not bad, but it does necessitate the introduction of a special support system to ensure that these teachers are either successful or quickly routed out of the system.

Numerous books and articles have been written about mentoring, so I will not go into detail here. However, I will spend some time outlining what I feel to be the most essential and doable elements of a mentoring program. The goals of mentoring programs, as they apply to new teachers, are to create an atmosphere of community, to provide expert training in the profession, to retain good teachers, and to provide support for the new teacher in times of self-doubt. This is called an *integrated professional culture* (Johnson et al., 2001, p. 6). Every teacher needs a critical friend, and that is the mentor.

Successful New-Teacher Mentoring Programs

Mentoring and induction programs work. The Career in Teaching plan in Rochester, New York, uses mentors and provides a career ladder for teachers; it increased the number of first-year teachers who returned for a second year from 69 percent in 1987 to 86 percent in 1999 (Kelly, 2001, p. 5). The new-teacher program at Leyden High School in Franklin Park, Illinois, has resulted in a first-year retention rate of 85–95 percent (Martin & Robbins, 1999, p. 33). Lafourche Parish, in Louisiana, reduced its teacher attrition rate from 51 percent to 15 percent almost immediately after introducing a new-teacher induction program in 1996. By 2002, the attrition rate in Lafourche Parish had dropped to 7 percent (Wong, 2002, p. 54).

There are numerous successful teacher induction programs, usually existing as part of a larger overall professional development plan. For instance, the San Diego Unified School District maintains a High Performance in Teaching and Learning Department (Sparks & Hirsh, 1997, p. 53). A central aspect of the district's professional development model is "job-embedded learning," and one example of this technique is its teacher mentoring program, which provides new teachers with assistance from both a mentor teacher and a university coach.

The Tucson Unified School District has a staff development department that

> coordinates the new-teacher induction process for the school system. New teachers meet monthly to address typical concerns. They spend part of each meeting in study groups facilitated by members of the teacher cadre. In addition, cadre members provide school-based support for new teachers. (Sparks & Hirsh, 1997, p. 59)

Selecting and Training the Effective Mentor

As discussed in the previous chapter, a great teacher is not necessarily also a great mentor. The skills are not the same. Adult learners are different from younger learners. Remember that new teachers are already credentialed, in some ways implying that they have already made the grade, unlike students encountering classes for the first time. For all these reasons, anyone wishing to be a mentor must pass through some screening and then undergo some training. Among the topics mentors need to understand and characteristics they need to have are "the role of the mentor; the needs, problems, and phases of beginning teachers; observation and feedback strategies; and effective teaching strategies" (Brooks, 1999, p. 55); "strong interpersonal skills, credibility with peers and administrators, a demonstrated eagerness and curiosity to learn, respect for multiple perspectives, and outstanding instructional practice" (Moir, Gless, & Baron, 1999, pp. 112–113).

The potential mentor begins by completing an application, as in Figure 3.1. This application should include some standard information, such as areas of expertise and years of experience. Then, the application should challenge the prospective mentor to convince the persons choosing the mentors that he or she is suitable for the position. Essay questions such as "Why do you want to be a mentor?" and "What qualities do you possess that would make you a successful mentor?" will help eliminate those teachers who simply want the stipend or who are just not ready for this position of responsibility. The teacher should be able to produce three letters from colleagues supporting the request to be a mentor. Finally, a committee of teachers and the principal should interview the candidates for mentoring. Ideally, enough acceptable applicants will have emerged to comprise a pool of mentors from which one can choose, as necessary, in any given year.

Those chosen to be mentors then need some specific training. Here, we begin to develop an economy of scale. In the last chapter, we spoke of training cooperating teachers to work with student interns. Much of that training would apply here as well. Mentors

FIGURE 3.1

Sample Mentor Application

MENTOR APPLICATION

Name: _____

Areas of Certification: _____

Years of Experience: _____

Have you ever been a mentor before? Please give details. _____

_____

_____

_____

_____

What experience or training do you have with adult learning? _____

_____

_____

_____

_____

Why do you wish to be a mentor?

(Attach separate sheets.)

What qualities do you possess that will make you a successful mentor?

(Attach separate sheets.)

FOR COMMITTEE MEMBERS:
Interview notes:

Final decision and reasons for it:

will have to know how to observe instruction accurately and percep-
tively. They will also have to be able to communicate what they
see with sensitivity, tact, and clarity. After all that, the task of the
mentor is to coach the new teacher in the development of his or
her skills and the refinement of techniques. At all times, the mentor
must maintain absolute confidentiality for this relationship to work.
More so than the relationship between the cooperating teacher
and intern, this relationship is similar to that between a master and
an apprentice. The master's job is to take the raw material of the
accepted novice and guide that new professional's growth to a stage
of independent competence.

Being a mentor is not a casual activity, and it is not for just anyone. That is why I would recommend a fairly rigorous method of
selection. A principal would not let just anybody coach basketball,
so why would he or she let just anybody become a mentor?

In 1998, a group of 56 Texas school districts belonging to a con-
sortium called the Region IV Educational Service Center anticipated
7,200 teaching vacancies for the next school year (Coppenhaver
& Schaper, 1999). With numbers like these, there was a real need for
good mentoring, which resulted in formal training for teacher mentors. For this program, "the heart of mentoring is supporting new
educators so that they *think* as a teacher thinks" (Coppenhaver &
Schaper, 1999, p. 64). Among the skills taught to mentors are
observing classrooms, reflecting with novices in conferences, articu-
lating the basic concepts of the profession, fostering professional
independence, and tactfully communicating classroom critique. All
this training is supported with a great deal of practice during a
three-day training program (Coppenhaver & Schaper, 1999).

The Effective Assignment of Mentors

The mentor's first responsibility is to provide a smooth transition
from preservice training to actual professional employment for the
new teacher. If the new teacher's first-year experience is not a satisfying one, if it is fraught with difficulty and disappointment, then
there is a good chance that that teacher will not return, and the

principal will be back in the position of having to fill the vacancy. Remember, because we have a teacher shortage, finding good teachers is not enough. Keeping them is also a must.

Therefore, if at all possible, the principal should assign mentors who have something in common with their mentees, specifically their field of expertise and grade level (Charkes, Cassidy, & Olson, 2001, p. 6). Although this matching is not absolutely necessary, it should be given careful attention. For instance, you would not do well to pair a new counselor with a classroom teacher or a new nurse with the head of the foreign language department. A study of induction programs found that "[a]lthough virtually all of the new teachers we interviewed had official mentors assigned by their districts, those mentors frequently taught in different schools, levels, or subjects, and meetings with them were intermittent and brief at best" (Johnson et al., 2001, p. 8). This mismatching is not helpful.

The pairing should be done as soon as possible. Ideally, weeks before the school year begins, the mentor will have written to his or her charge. In this way, the relationship can already be under way before the first day of school, and at least one familiar face will be waiting for the new teacher. An English teacher expressed her feelings about this relationship in this way:

> It was incredibly comforting to receive a letter from a fellow English teacher, welcoming me to the school community and encouraging me to contact her if I had any questions or needed help in any areas. I didn't feel the need to contact her before school started, but once the school year began I turned to her a lot for advice and information. (Harvey et al., 1998, p. 141)

During the days before school opens, the mentor can do much to ease the entry of the new teacher. We often take for granted much practical information about a geographic area and leave new people to fend for themselves. For instance, if the new teacher is moving into the area, he or she may want to know about housing, doctors, dentists, shopping, entertainment, public transportation, and the like. Remember, we want to make that first year as successful as possible. A new teacher has enough to worry about without wondering where to go for the best pizza. Area maps are good for this kind of thing.

Make entry into the profession an occasion for celebration. A day or two before the experienced staff returns, arrange some kind of activity for mentors and new teachers, including a luncheon and activities to get to know one another. Make the new teachers' first impression of the school a positive one, and let them know that you care about their welfare. Later, at the first teachers' meeting, go out of your way to introduce new teachers to the group, making sure to give some background on each one. Allow some time at the meeting for casual conversation so that new teachers can begin to meet and know their colleagues. Every step of the way, new teachers must know that they are cared for and are not going to be left on their own to struggle alone in the classroom. The principal and school should support new teachers as they would any vulnerable person.

> The principal, mentor, and other support persons must establish rapport and build trust with the beginning teacher at the earliest opportunity. Rapport can be established through open communication, clarifying and dignifying the beginner's concerns, and accepting the new teacher as a colleague. The new teacher's trust can be earned by displaying competence and professionalism as a support person, maintaining confidentiality, keeping commitments, and helping her experience success during the initial days of teaching. (Gordon & Maxey, 2000, p. 60)

Supporting the Induction and Mentoring Process

The daily schedule will no doubt present challenges for the principal in designing time for the mentor and new teacher to work together. The smaller the school, the fewer the scheduling options. Principals will have to be creative, thinking outside the typical parameters of scheduling. In the best situation, the mentor and new teacher would have teaching schedules that allow them to observe one another and to have extended conversations. Several approaches are possible (see Figure 3.2).

First, the principal and others in the system will have to be ready to step up and cover classes to allow observations and conferences

---

FIGURE 3.2

National Best Practices for Addressing the Issue of Time to Mentor

1. Releasing mentors and new teachers from noninstructional duties

2. Scheduling common preparation time for mentors and new teachers

3. Providing opportunities for mentors and new teachers to team teach

4. Drawing on central office staff or building administrators as regular roving substitutes

5. Using faculty from institutions of higher education as substitutes, generally as part of a professional development school design

Source: From Brennan et al., as cited in Charkes et al. (2001, pp. 14–15).

---

to occur. In the previous chapter, we saw the possibility of using the administration, paraprofessionals, or substitutes for this purpose. General inservice time may also provide opportunities for new teachers and mentors to work together. Other teachers may have to step in to help as well. The mentoring of a new teacher is really the responsibility of the entire system, which should have as part of its mission the maintenance and nurturing of high standards in new generations of members of its professional ranks. All educational professionals are gatekeepers, and this role must be part of the institutional culture. "The success of school-based induction programs hinges on how teachers work together, and the principal can play a central role in establishing faculty norms and facilitating interaction among teachers with various levels of experience" (Johnson et al., 2001, p. 6).

If at all possible, the new teacher and mentor should be on the same teaching team, in the same department, in the same grade level, or somehow connected in their day-to-day assignments. If they could share supervisory duties, the mentee would not feel so lonely while trying to establish authority with students. If all else fails, the principal may have to assign a reduced load to the mentor or relieve the mentor, mentee, or both from supervisory duties to make the necessary time available for them to work together. If the principal has created the atmosphere of collaboration that comes with a professional development school, then these kinks in the schedule should be accepted as part of the job rather than jealously perceived as privilege for some. This is a tricky point to negotiate, and the principal has to be careful to apportion the rewards and obligations fairly across the faculty and staff. Everyone must learn to accept and see quality of instruction as the number one priority of the school.

If all works as it should, then mentors and new teachers will be able to observe each other's classes and have time to discuss professional issues every week. The mentor must be compensated for this work, which is both difficult and time-consuming. A reduced teaching load, fewer supervisory duties, stipends, or some combination of all three will be an absolute necessity to preserve the professionalism of the mentor. Teachers' time is valuable, and their expertise is not something to be taken for granted. There may be times when a teacher offers to help pro bono; in fact, I hope that this would be the case. However, the principal cannot allow such offers to be the rule; they must be the exception when no other solution can be found.

Support Groups for Mentors and New Teachers

As with the preservice programs, both mentors and new teachers will need support within their own groups. Again, I would suggest that mentors meet regularly, at least once each month, to discuss the mentoring process. "Mentors need ongoing organizational, technical, and affective support" (Gordon & Maxey, 2000, p. 46). New teachers should also meet regularly to discuss common difficulties and triumphs, and to make suggestions for improving their experience and training. A new-teacher seminar, not dissimilar to the seminar for interns, would help mentees through some of the particularly difficult tasks of teaching for the first time. What follows is a sample of sessions that one might find in such a seminar:

- *Classroom management:* How does a teacher establish control of a class? What are some effective classroom arrangements? What are some effective intervention techniques? Are there particular rules and sanctions that are part of school policy? Whom does the teacher see for help, and where does he or she send problem students? When is it time to contact a parent? How does a teacher establish positive relationships with students without becoming a "buddy"?

- *Parent conferences:* How does a teacher set up a parent conference? How does one handle an irate parent or one who challenges the teacher's authority? How can the teacher phrase bad news without being offensive? How can a teacher avoid becoming defensive? Does this school follow certain protocols?

- *Methodology:* What are various ways of presenting information in class? How does a teacher keep students engaged? Are students allowed to go outside? What is too much noise? How does one set up effective group work? Is lecturing all right to do? Can students be up and moving about, or should they primarily be working at their seats?

- *Lesson planning:* What does a good lesson plan look like? How is a 45-minute class different from a block format class? Will supervisors be looking for specific characteristics in the lesson plans? Will the plans have to be handed in?

- *Nuts and bolts of the system:* Who is in charge of what? Who is in charge of whom? What are the policies that define procedures in such cases as harassment, discipline, evaluation, and emergency situations?

I could go on at some length here, but the idea is, obviously, to anticipate what a new teacher needs to know and then take steps to avoid a mishap before it occurs, thus alleviating a good deal of anxiety and difficulty. "Well-matched mentors, curriculum guidance, collaborative lesson planning, peer observation, and inspired leadership all support new teachers in ways that recruitment incentives never can" (Johnson et al., 2001, p. 6).

Be particularly sure that a new teacher understands how he or she will be supervised and evaluated. We insist that students understand teacher expectations, so the least we can do is afford the same courtesy to new professionals. I will discuss supervision and evaluation at greater length in the chapter on inservice professional development.

Teaching Assignments

A typical practice in teaching is to give the new person the least desirable assignment, usually a class that has had poor academic performance and discipline problems. One teacher put it this way:

> Nothing will cause burn-out in a new teacher quicker than giving him or her all freshmen, or all remedial, or all discipline problems. If anything, these new teachers need time to test their new wings, to try out their knowledge in an elective area. They bring with them freshness and enthusiasm straight from the world of academe. Tap into their resources—don't let them go to waste. (Harvey et al., 1998, p. 142)

Assigning classes purely on the basis of seniority, with the best going to the most veteran teachers, is entirely inappropriate. If a principal wants to ensure that a new teacher has a difficult and disappointing first teaching experience, then employing this practice would be the way to do it. By rights, the most experienced and talented teacher should handle the most challenging students. "If we took new teachers seriously as learners, we would not expect them to do the same job or have the same skills as experienced teachers" (Feiman-Nemser et al., 1999, p. 7).

This method of assigning classes may, however, make people feel as if they are being punished for years of service. I suggest that, at the very least, new-teacher assignments should be primarily classes that present average challenge. If novice teachers must teach more difficult groups, the principal would be wise to establish a teaming situation in that case. I would also recommend teaming if the new teacher is assigned a highly advanced class. Those sharp, competitive students can be just as difficult as their uninspired counterparts. At any rate, the principal or department head needs to distribute classes equitably, and not in a way that crushes the new teacher immediately. I cannot emphasize enough that we are trying to attract and *retain* good teachers, not immediately burn them out.

Nontraditional Teachers

The nontraditional teacher will present a special case. Someone who has just left another profession to become a teacher, a local chemist who has been hired on a waiver, or someone who has been certified by some alternative route such as peer review will bring a wide range of experience and readiness to the classroom. Some of these teachers may be older than the typical first-year professional and consequently no longer used to being in a novice position. You cannot treat a 50-year-old new teacher in the same way as you would a 21-year-old new teacher. Think of the difference between teaching an elementary school student how to play the piano and teaching a 40-year-old how to play the piano. The younger teacher is more liable to have a greater tolerance for failure and the need to start over than is the adult who has already been established in life, with a family and perhaps a previously successful career. On the other hand, the younger teacher tends to be more egocentric and idealistic, while the older individual tends to be more reflective and realistic. For a fuller discussion of adult learning stages, I recommend Chapter 4 ("Contrasting Optimal Adult Development with Actual Teacher Development: Clues for Supervisory Practice") in Glickman's (1985) *Supervision of Instruction: A Developmental Approach* (pp. 43–73).

There may be serious gaps in the training of nontraditional teachers. Remember, these are not the people who came through your teaching intern program. On the bright side, they may bring different, valuable experiences and deeper life wisdom that can be helpful to others, especially idealistic younger teachers. A good principal will recognize and capture these skills, asking the nontraditional teachers to share their knowledge with others, perhaps even leading some of the new-teacher seminars. At the same time, they may need greater assistance than their younger peers in such areas as lesson planning, teaching methodologies, classroom management, technology integration in the classroom, and student evaluation. Remember, also, that new teachers have been trained in the latest instructional methods, which they can share with their veteran partners.

Retaining Is More Cost-Effective Than Recruiting

If the principal has done his or her work well in creating a positive climate, then the school will feel like a family, with members looking out for one another. New teachers must be welcomed and integrated into this family. The more they feel a sense of appreciation and belonging, the greater the likelihood that they will stay after their first year.

Retention is more cost-effective than recruitment. For example, California's Beginning Teacher Support and Assessment program "has been able to demonstrate through local retention studies that is it more effective to invest in BTSA—resulting in a 93 percent retention rate—than to spend money on recruiting each year" (Schultz, 1999, p. 100).

Now that you have done all that you can to retain new teachers, it is time to think about the long run. Teaching still has one of the highest overall turnover rates of any profession. The next step is to extend the idea of a professional development school to everyone in the institution. Ongoing professional development, developmental supervision, peer supervision, and teacher empowerment will be crucial aspects of this next phase of teacher retention.

4

Vision and Hiring:
The Keys to Effective Change

Half the challenge in coming to terms with the teacher shortage is finding ways to stem the tide of young teachers who leave the profession in their first few years. We would need far fewer new teachers if we could hire the most suitable people in the first place and then hold onto them.

A consideration here is the philosophy of your school. How can you know who will fit well with your institution if you do not know who you are? What does your school stand for? What is its collective attitude toward children, teaching, learning, professional development, and discipline? To match new hires to your school, you need to know what you are matching, and that means you need a clear statement of institutional identity. If new teachers find that the school complements their own style and beliefs, then those teachers are likely to be comfortable and productive, and they have a good chance of getting their professional needs satisfied by the school's climate, practices, and beliefs. Obviously, such teachers will be more apt to remain in the profession and in that particular school than those who do not fit in with the school's value system and feel out of place, disillusioned, or frustrated.

Philosophy

The words *vision*, *philosophy*, and *mission* are tossed around quite a bit in educational facilities. We often spend more time developing such statements than actually applying them. We can spend hours debating what these terms mean and how they differ from one another. For instance, psychologist Charles Garfield defines mission as "an image of a desired state of affairs that inspires action" (Oakley & Krug, 1991, p. 170). Carl E. Larson and Frank M. LaFasto use the words *goal*, *purpose*, and *mission* more or less interchangeably (Oakley & Krug, 1991, p. 170). Peter Block defines vision as the "deepest expression of what we want. It is the preferred future, a desirable state, an ideal state, an expression of optimism. It expresses the spiritual and idealistic side of our nature. It is a dream created in our waking hours of how we would like our lives to be" (Oakley & Krug, 1991, p. 172).

Rather than spending time on the details of definitions of words that can be virtually indistinguishable, we can instead realize that what we need is a statement that explains who we are, what we do, why we do it, and how we do it. An excellent statement will actually show what these concepts look like, not merely list them. It will clearly define and direct institutional behavior. Unfortunately, according to Carlson and Ducharme (1987), "clear mission statements lead to clear purposes which lead to clear results. . . . Public schools are frequently not characterized by clear, carefully constructed mission statements" (p. 1).

Creating a Useful Mission Statement

Perhaps the process of setting direction would be easier if we defined it in terms of some simple questions:

- What do we want students to know and be able to do?
- What methods will we use to help students achieve these goals?
- How do we want students and teachers to act?
- How should we treat students and teachers?

The first time I was in a position to hire, I did a mediocre job. In retrospect, I realize that this was the result of not having answers to these questions. The school had no coherent direction or methodology, which led to a climate of isolation, unhappiness, mistrust, and lack of collaborative effort. The result for me was that I was not clear on why I was hiring someone and whether the person would fit in with the faculty, the department, or the community. I could speak only of my own philosophy and attitude toward teachers, students, and learning, but I could not speak for the institution. Because my own ideas did not necessarily match those of a majority of the staff or even a few of my colleagues, I had no yardstick with which to measure the potential teacher's suitability to work as a member of the faculty.

Too often, when I found someone who seemed solid, someone with whom I could communicate well, the story ended unhappily. Because I did not represent the school, the new teacher soon found out that the ideas we agreed about and the positive relationship we had established did not necessarily apply to the rest of the institution. The result was unhappiness, frustration, and often bitterness.

In contrast to this situation, I later found myself hiring for a new school that was just establishing its belief system. In this case, I knew what we were all about, what we believed, and how we worked. Not everyone in the school agreed with my perceptions, but by being in the position to hire a large number of staff members and being clear myself as to what I wanted the school to be, I was in a strong position to build a faculty that would complement my vision. As indicated earlier, it is much easier to hire people who fit your vision than to try to change people already established in their beliefs.

By now you have probably noticed that for someone discussing vision, I am using the word *I* too often. However, who is the keeper of the vision if not the principal? Who is charged with supporting that vision, cheerleading the community as it strives to achieve it, and filtering out that which does not fit with it? Too often, philosophies or vision statements are created by well-meaning committees, voted on by apathetic faculties, and then shelved until the next round of accreditation. Someone needs to be charged with keeping the vision, and that person is the principal. For that reason, I see the principal as the major player in developing and guarding the vision, but certainly not in isolation.

Vision development demands input and investment by many people representing various constituencies. This is the work of the committee. A group of people can solicit, collate, and organize large amounts of information from various members of the district, including parents, businesspeople, the central administration, the school board, teachers, the general community, and students. At this point, the process might benefit from becoming a bit more auto-cratic. Given all the data, the principal, perhaps with the assistance of one or two others, can craft a statement that best addresses every-one's concerns. This statement must be brief, clear, simple, and understandable. Statements written by committees often lack these qualities. Although many people contribute ideas, the actual writing is better done by one person for the sake of clarity and consistent voice. The mission statement must also define everything that hap-pens in the school. Obviously, it is of enormous importance. The first attempt at the statement is circulated to all parties for com-ment, revised, and circulated again, with this process continuing until most people are satisfied with the tone and direction. In this way, the principal may control the process, but everyone is heard several times.

Let's revisit the questions listed earlier and see how they might lead to a vision or philosophy.

1. *What do we want students to know and be able to do?* This ques-tion is clearly related to curriculum and leads to several important issues. Do we want students to know certain facts? Do we want them to know certain processes? Is research important? Are problem solving and experimentation important? What knowledge and skills will best prepare them for the future, and how will we evaluate our students' progress?

These questions usually lead to some boilerplate language about being a good citizen, being prepared to meet the challenges of the future, and protecting the planet. Although few people, if any, would argue with these values, they are too vague to make much difference in the day-to-day activity of a school. They are not defining. A statement more likely to set a direction would be something like "We want our students to leave high school prepared to understand the world around them, formulate clear and intelligent opinions, and express those opinions with clarity, sincerity, and persuasiveness."

This statement includes the idea of the traditional curriculum, but it translates that curriculum into action—understanding and expressing that understanding through taking a stance on issues. Assessment is embedded in the statement. Students will be asked to present their ideas and opinions, supported by facts, in a persuasive manner. These are the skills of informed citizenship in a democratic society.

2. *What methods will we use to help students achieve these goals?* Now we move into the arena of pedagogy. How are we going to teach? Again, we can throw around buzzwords such as *cooperative learning, brain based, student centered,* or *constructivist,* but these terms represent large concepts, each deserving an entire book in itself. They may drive instruction, but they do not necessarily drive a common conception of instruction. A more basic approach could be to say, "Students will be at the center of our instruction, their learning styles defining our teaching approaches." This statement moves us away from fads (not that what I listed above are fads) and toward a specific philosophy of teaching. We will tailor our teaching to the ways students learn.

3. *How do we want students and teachers to act?* This brings us into the realm of climate. Here, we usually hear such words as *respect, tolerance,* and *appreciation of diversity.* Once more, a better approach would be to define specific actions, not broad ideals. What specifically will teachers and students be doing, and what will it look like? A possible statement might be "Members of our school community will listen to one another respectfully, protect one another's personal space, consider various points of view on issues, and work collaboratively." *Respect, diversity,* and *tolerance* all reside in this sentence, but the sentence tells people what these concepts look like in action rather than merely offering abstract terms to consider.

4. *How should we treat teachers and students?* Finally, we are moving into the area of personal relationships. Relationship building is central to good teaching. Students and staff need a safe, friendly, supportive environment to perform at top levels. How can we put this in the vision statement in such a way as to help people create these relationships? One way might be to say, "We all must look out for one another, thus creating a safe, caring environment in which to work and play." It is not enough to tell people what you want them to do. You have to give them the tools—the actual vision, if you will—to illustrate the state you want to achieve.

Now we can put our vision statement together:

> We want our students to leave high school prepared to understand the world around them, formulate clear and intelligent opinions, and express those opinions with clarity, sincerity, and persuasiveness. Students will be at the center of our instruction, their learning styles defining our teaching approaches. Members of our school community will listen to one another respectfully, protect one another's personal space, consider various points of view on issues, and work collaboratively. We all must look out for one another, thus creating a safe, caring environment in which to work and play.

Contrast the clear, action-defining character of this philosophy to another one, quoted from a public school handbook. I was a member of the committee that wrote it, about a decade ago:

> Trust, kindness, and respect must govern us all in this educational community. Our community includes students, parents, staff, school board members, and citizens. Working together and taking risks are part of a successful educational community. Our school is a learning environment in which each person can grow. Each person has unique developmental needs which the school addresses. We encourage academic excellence. We prepare students to be well educated citizens, participating in a changing and interdependent world. A successful school community celebrates the success of each individual. This Philosophy Statement is a "Living Document," open to revision according to its own standards.

Notice that both statements are about the same length. Also observe that all of the right words and phrases are there, such as *respect, taking risks, learning environment, unique developmental needs, academic excellence, educated citizens,* and *capable of participating.* However, in the second example, these terms are not conveyed in such a way as to give the reader a clear picture of what they would look like when implemented.

Using the Philosophy as a Basis for Hiring

Unlike many philosophies or vision statements that I have read, the one I have constructed in response to the four questions forms the concrete basis for selecting teaching candidates with specific qualities, training, attitudes, and beliefs. The principal is going to be held accountable for the success or failure of those he or she hires. Therefore, after the major ideas of the philosophy emerge from the larger community conversations, it is the principal's job to convert that language into usable terms. The idea of vision needs to apply at all levels. It should define how boards select central administrators; how central administrators choose building administrators; how building administrators select teachers and other building staff; and how board members, administrators, teachers, and students interact.

I have spent a good deal of time on this idea of vision or philosophy, and by now some of you may be wondering when I will live up to my own requirements and demonstrate the philosophy in action. As we return to our central themes, the attraction and retention of teachers as a method of combating the teacher shortage, we can see how this discussion has direct application. We need to attract and hire people who will fit in with our organizations, find kindred spirits, have success, and, therefore, be less likely to leave. For example, during one of my principalships, I had the opportunity to hire 13 teachers over a couple of years. Of these, only three left, and of those, one found a job closer to home.

Although I always hired by committee, I also always held a preinterview with each prospective candidate. During this session, I did most of the talking. I would mercilessly bombard the teacher with everything that was going to be a particular challenge at the school. At that point, I would ask whether there was any reason to continue the interview. If the person was still interested, I moved into the area of philosophy, methodology, attitude toward students, and responsibilities to parents. Again, I would ask whether the candidate was still interested. Those who remained interested or even excited about the position created a pool of candidates who were well suited and likely to work out. At that point, we scheduled an interview with the hiring committee. See Figure 4.1 for some ideas of what one can learn from a first interview based on a vision statement.

A teacher new to your school should find no surprises. In the first interview, I would be brutally honest about the student population, its problems, and its needs. Several first-year teachers decided to discontinue the discussion then and there, and I was glad they did. Rather than being disappointed in them, I assured them that my respect for them had increased as a result of their honesty. We both wanted a good experience for the teacher, the students, and the school. There is nothing wrong with realizing that one is not well suited to a particular position. In fact, it is better for everyone to find this out before the hiring is done, not after. Many schools exist,

---

FIGURE 4.1

What Are You Looking for in a First Interview?

Attitude	Pedagogy	Learner	Management	Collaborator
• Likes kids	• Student centered	• Reflective thinker	• Treats students with respect	• Can work with others
• Positive	• Multiple techniques	• Comfortable with risks	• Can keep students engaged	• Can flow with a situation
• Flexible	• Can match technique to student	• Can fail and try again	• Puts students at the center	• Willing to share
• Supportive	• Good knowledge base in field	• Accepts criticism	• Can handle difficult students	• Respectful of others
• Understands need to work with parents		• Desire to learn and improve	• Handles most of own problems	

each with a different institutional personality. Candidate and school need to complement each other.

The vision has some specific things to say about pedagogy. New teachers need to know how teaching is done at your school. If we use the first philosophy statement presented earlier, then we can let prospective teachers know some of what will be required of them. For instance, are they ready to match their teaching style to the learning styles of their students? Do they have a sufficient repertoire of methods to create rich, student-centered environments? Are they willing to take the time to prepare and deliver a sample lesson?

A crucial area to investigate concerns the candidate's attitude toward students. There is no reason to hire any person who does not like kids. If a person does not enjoy the students, then he or she does not belong in a classroom. There is nothing more depressing than watching someone who does not like children working with them all day long.

Questions about discipline elicit creativity, a sense of respect for students, and tolerance for tough situations. You will also want to ask questions about pedagogy. Depending on your school, this approach could mean looking for someone with knowledge of multiple intelligences, constructivism, brain research, specialized reading techniques, and the like. Can this person work with others, not just getting along, but actually collaborating? Does this person share your vision about education and children?

Finally, does the candidate possess the necessary characteristics of a good learner: reflectiveness, curiosity, risk taking, desire to grow, willingness to fail and try again? If these qualities are present, but the candidate does not have all the skills you want, you will be able to train him or her. As long as the basic attitude is right, and the teacher has the capacity and willingness to learn the required techniques, then all is well.

As you can see from Figure 4.1, I have tried to translate my sample philosophy into a table of issues to probe in an interview. Obviously, the table could be filled in an infinite number of ways, depending on the school. The objective is to be consistent in hiring, so that you build a cadre of like-minded people. This characterization does not mean people who all agree on everything, but it does mean a group of people who share certain characteristics, attitudes, and habits of mind.

If you want to retain good teachers, then you need to hire teachers who will be content in the school environment you provide. Candidates who do not like the vision drop out of the race. Those left, in theory, possess the characteristics you are looking for. If you have partnered with a teacher training institution, then you have an even better chance of finding a good match, because you will have been working with potential candidates in your school for as many as four years (more on this later).

The Second Interview

Once you are reasonably sure that you have candidates who are well-matched to the school's vision, you can set up the second interview. This time, a team of teachers should conduct the interview, for two reasons. First, these are the people who will have to work with this new colleague, so who better to know whether such collaboration will be possible? Second, the process honors and therefore empowers teachers to choose the new candidate. As discussed elsewhere in this book, teachers, as professionals, should be part of the gatekeeping function that decides who will and who will not become a teacher. This approach improves climate, morale, professionalism, and esteem.

Sample Interview Questions Based on a Vision Statement

The following is the vision statement again, this time followed by a series of interview questions that might be drawn from it. These questions could be used in a first or second interview.

The Vision

We want our students to leave high school prepared to understand the world around them, formulate clear and intelligent opinions, and express those opinions with clarity, sincerity, and persuasiveness. Students will be at the center of our instruction, their learning styles defining our teaching approaches. Members of our school community will listen to one another respectfully, protect one another's personal space, consider various points of view on issues, and work collaboratively. We all must look out for one another, thus creating a safe, caring environment in which to work and play.

This vision statement leads to the following interview questions:

1. How do you feel when a student challenges your opinion or statement of fact?
2. What are the three most important skills or ideas all students should learn?
3. What skills are necessary for successful participation in a democracy?
4. In what classes should communication skills be taught?
5. What would you say is an optimal ratio of student to teacher talk in a class?
6. What does respect look like?
   a. Between teachers and students?
   b. Between students and students?
   c. Between teachers and teachers?
   d. Between teachers and parents?
   e. Between teachers and administrators?
7. How can teachers help each other?
8. Tell me about a time when you felt ignorant, uninformed, or stupid. What did you do about the situation?
9. How do you deal with the diversity of types of learners in a class?
10. Who has had the most influence on your thinking and philosophy?
11. How do you take care of yourself?
12. What are the steps you would take with a student whose acting-out behavior is escalating?
13. How do you deal with people who disagree with the beliefs you hold strongly?
14. What have you done that you are most proud of?
15. What was your greatest failure and what did you do about it?

16. Briefly explain at least three different teaching methodologies. Do you have a favorite one?
17. Why do you want to work here?
18. What do you have to offer the school community?
19. What do you hope to gain from working here?
20. What are your career goals?

The Teacher Shortage as an Opportunity

A clear vision and hiring on the basis of that vision lie at the very heart of creating a successful school. If the teacher shortage provides us with the opportunity to actually build faculties of like-minded people, people who buy into the way a particular school does things, then the shortage may actually offer us the greatest chance to effect positive and enduring change in education in 100 years. As you well know, trying to motivate a large, settled faculty to change is extraordinarily difficult. However, if you need to hire a sufficient number of new teachers to create a critical mass, then you have the chance to actually shape the school.

Inservice Programming: A Dynamic Professional Atmosphere

You have now attracted good teachers to your school and ensured that they have had a successful first year. How are you going to keep these well-trained, carefully selected new teachers? You have invested a good deal of time, effort, and funds to this point, so it is imperative to maintain your new faculty members, or all of your efforts will have been for naught. If we assume that the kind of teachers you want, and presumably the kind you have hired, are most content in a dynamic, growing, exciting, professional environment, then the next consideration would have to be inservice programs that support such an environment.

New teachers flourish in an integrated professional culture that encourages teacher collaboration across experience levels, but veteran teachers also benefit from such professional exchange. In addition to the obvious rewards of mentoring for both parties, new teachers often possess skills—such as the ability to integrate technology into the curriculum or interpret data from standards-based assessments—that veteran teachers need. Schools that gear professional development to both the ongoing induction of new teachers and the continual renewal of veteran teachers serve all educators well—thus enabling them to serve all their students well. (Johnson & Kardos, 2002, p. 16)

Components of Successful Inservice Programs

We have already looked at some inservice opportunities through the lenses of preservice and induction programs, both of which provided veteran teachers with new professional roles and responsibilities, as well as the attendant training. However, one would hope that a professional organization would have a larger, ongoing atmosphere of professional development, continuing to challenge teachers to learn and grow. Once again, a hospital environment provides a model. A typical practice in hospitals is something called "grand rounds." This term indicates a regularly scheduled time when all or part of the professional staff gathers to listen to a lecture delivered by one of their own or an outside expert. Although I would not recommend such a static form of inservice training, I would take a page from the hospital book and suggest that a regular system of inservice programming be built into the fabric of the institution.

I believe it is necessary to get beyond the typical inservice model. This model is one in which several days each year are set aside for teacher training, often in the form of a speaker, a workshop, time for parent conferences, or some other valuable but limited program. A common complaint is that there is little follow-up, no coaching, no extended postdiscussion. The innovation dies.

What I am proposing instead is that, in addition to the days set aside for inservice training, principals develop with their staffs a model for *continuous* inservice programming, one in which training, substantive conversation, and idea exchanges take place every day. Professional growth becomes part of the fabric of the institution, not something that happens on three or four special days. More specifically:

> Implementation of the [new] practice is guided by what we know about the change process. It begins with acquiring descriptive information and a clear picture for both teachers and administrators of how it will affect

their lives in the classroom and the school. Then "how-to-do-it" training is conducted, followed by practice, some with coaching. Training in small increments rather than all at once is preferred, so parts can be mastered one at a time and problems dealt with as they come up. At least a year of follow-up support is needed; this may include problem-solving gatherings, in-class demonstrations and assistance, and materials and logistical help. At the end of the year, depending on the practice and the progress, different kinds of sessions can be planned that focus on evaluation of progress and refinement of the use of the practice. (Loucks-Horsley et al., 1987, p. 57)

The National Staff Development Council (NSDC) recommends professional development programming that involves organizing teachers into adult learning communities whose goals align with school and district goals. The NSDC also points out that good professional development requires skillful school and district leaders to guide continuous instructional improvement and the necessary resources to support adult learning and collaboration (NSDC, 2001).

Inservice programs need to be honest. If you do not plan to follow up on the ideas presented or practiced, then why bother introducing them in the first place? Real inservice programming means devoting staff training to one or two ideas that will be pursued in depth, perhaps for more than one year. "The school and/or district needs to be sure that structures are in place to continue to nurture teachers' use of the practice. Unfortunately, this rarely happens" (Loucks-Horsley et al., 1987, p. 57). The training ought to have some value and meaning to the people who are receiving it. If the material does not mean anything to the audience, and if the staff knows that there will be no follow-up or accountability, then once again, time, money, and effort are wasted in the process. As Scherer (2002) points out:

Derisive stories about the worst professional development encountered are easy to come by in education. . . . That traditional professional development has not always been meaningful is an understatement. At the same time, relevant professional development has never been more important. (p. 5)

Where does such meaningful inservice programming come from? Teachers. Ask teachers what they want to learn, what they need to learn, what they feel is valuable to learn. Once you know the answers to these questions, you can begin to design, in concert with the faculty or a committee of the faculty, an inservice program that works on multiple levels. In addition to the major themes for the year, there can also be smaller, specialized programs for those interested. Grade-level teams may be responsible for some of their own inservice training. Individual teachers should have their own professional goals. You can devote the majority of faculty meeting time to substantive educational issues. Save the arguments over whether to allow students to wear hats for some other time.

To begin with, a good principal will survey his or her staff to determine what their needs are. When we teach our students, doesn't best practice suggest that we use their natural interests and current knowledge levels as points of entry for various disciplines? Why would we not do the same for teachers? You may be surprised by the results. I worked in a rural district in which the schools were small and geographically far apart. Several of the schools had only one teacher for each grade level or discipline area. Some schools had multigrade classrooms. When I surveyed the district with a questionnaire, I found that the number one request for inservice programming was time and opportunity for teachers of the same grade or subject area to talk with one another. What a remarkably simple idea, one that would not be accomplished by gathering everyone together to listen to an inspirational speaker. However, by taking a few hours from a couple of the scheduled inservice days, teachers could meet. The cost would be minimal, the teacher empowerment would be great, and something of substance could be accomplished, such as curriculum work.

Listen to teachers. Don't decide their needs for them. I would advise any principal to work with an inservice committee of teachers and other staff members to develop programs for the school. The results of my own work of surveying teachers and planning with an inservice committee in the system just described resulted in the program printed at the end of the chapter in Figure 5.6 (pp. 68–69).

Develop and Use Local Expertise

A key element in the aforementioned program was the use of local teachers. Building inner capacity is a means of honoring teachers as professionals with something to say. This approach, then, is another way to hold onto the best teachers: Treat them with the respect they deserve as educated, dedicated professionals. The bonus is that using local expertise is considerably less expensive than using outside experts, and local individuals remain in the area for follow-up or questions long after the initial presentation.

At other times, subjects for inservice work will come from analysis of test scores or other performance data, sometimes from mandates issued by the state or federal government. In any case, know why you are doing what you are doing, and invite others to plan with you. If you have no substantive program to fill the time, then let teachers fill it with their own work, with curriculum work, or with discussion and idea exchanges. All of this can be documented to ensure that real work goes on, which should satisfy the administration and the public as well. I will discuss this topic at greater length later in this chapter.

Daily, Embedded Inservice Programming

Imagine no inservice days and no expensive outside presenters. Instead, picture a system that devotes one half day every week, or perhaps every other week, to teachers working together as a staff, all year long. Such a three-hour block of time, used strategically and intelligently, could provide more professional growth than ever before. Let's take some time to examine in detail what this kind of time might mean to a school's professional atmosphere.

First, administrative matters should be reduced, as much as possible, to memos. How many times have you seen an entire meeting eaten up over debate on whether to allow students to travel in two directions on the stairs or to have an up staircase and a down staircase? This is an area in which a principal should not be afraid to be unilateral and directive. Certainly solicit, in writing, teachers' opinions. Then, after having read them and thought about the matter, make a decision. Such debates use up precious time and energy. Management decisions can be made by management. Educational decisions should be made by educators. Learn to play these two roles appropriately. Your faculty meeting time is sacred time, reserved for discussion of teaching and learning issues.

I would say that each three-hour meeting could be divided into four major areas: celebrating, sharing, training, and practice. Each meeting probably would not allow the same amount of time for each segment; the time would vary depending on topics for examination, deadlines, special events, and the like. Imagine a meeting set up in this way: First, teachers would have an opportunity to announce good news. Perhaps Billy finally passed the state math assessment. Mrs. Jones's class received a letter from the museum complimenting them on their behavior. Mr. Smith's students completed the welcome mural in the front hallway of the school. The next short segment of the meeting would involve sharing. Sharing could include making announcements, pointing out problem areas in the school to be corrected (there is always a bottleneck in the C wing between periods 5 and 6), and requesting assistance (does anyone have materials on Norse mythology?). These are not points for discussion. The balance of the session may then be devoted to training and guided practice or application of new skills and information. Finally, someone should always keep a carefully written journal of the meeting as a record to document what has been accomplished and for reference later in the year. Figure 5.1 outlines a half-day inservice schedule.

The basic model is fairly simple. One can vary it in a number of ways. For instance, there may be a reason to break the faculty into groups, such as grade level, curricular area, special project, or planning. This grouping would allow for the kind of teamwork and preparation that is essential for a coordinated program. Also, various groups may be at different stages regarding the year's professional development theme (some just getting started, some in progress, and some evaluating their work). In each case, part of or the entire meeting might be devoted to group work, with some time left for each group to report to the whole assembly.

FIGURE 5.1

Three-Hour Inservice Plan

Half-Day Meeting Outline

1:00—Announcements/calendar

1:15—Sharing and Good News
    Events
    Accomplishments
    Who needs what?
    Upcoming activities

1:45—Pressing Issues
    Discipline
    Schedule
    Problem spots
    Quick decisions

2:00—Curriculum and Pedagogy
    Training
    Practice
    Application
    Follow-up
    Critique
    Student work

4:00—Adjourn

Having teachers work in groups is a critical part of building accumulated professional knowledge, according to James Stigler, a professor of psychology at the University of California–Los Angeles. Stigler has studied teacher professional development, coauthoring with James Hiebert the book *The Teaching Gap: Best Ideas from the World's Teachers for Improving Education in the Classroom* (1999). Stigler notes that teachers are learning all the time from experience, but there is no clear process for individual educators to share their knowledge with each other. He suggests that "we need to create contexts in which collaborative work can be sustained" (Willis, 2002, p. 8).

At times, the principal may want to devote the entire time to teachers' working individually. This would be a natural use of the session when the staff is preparing report cards or holding parent conferences. At first, some monitoring of the situation may be required, but with time and honesty comes trust, and then "checking up" on people will not be necessary, especially if the principal has established a professional development climate, as we have discussed before. In such a school, people thrive on their work, valuing blocks of time they can use to advance their individual projects or assignments. At other times, there may be a reason to use the whole meeting for a single, group purpose, such as evaluating student portfolios or other general assessment tools. Ideally, the principal and staff will plan ahead of time, even outlining the agendas for half a dozen consecutive half days at once. Figure 5.2 illustrates planning for a month of inservice days.

These half days certainly move a school in the direction of continuous professional development, but we can focus in more tightly as we view the institutional operation. For some time, the team structure has been a staple of middle school philosophy. More and more schools are extending this idea to other grade levels for numerous reasons. Teachers can coordinate instruction, share information about students, and generally support one another. In particular, new teachers can quickly find a home, a comfort zone, when they become part of an established team.

Successful and Productive Teams

Simply having teams is not enough; one must also provide the teams with regular meeting times. If the members of a team cannot plan together, then they are a team in name only. Regular meeting time without productive work is equally inadequate. By establishing a format, guidelines, and expectations for team meetings, the concept of professional development can be brought to the level of daily team activity. For instance, the week might be divided for various purposes:

Monday:	Team planning
Tuesday:	Parent meetings; team planning
Wednesday:	Special education meetings; team planning
Thursday:	Team planning
Friday:	Meet with principal; team planning

The depth of the work envisioned here probably cannot be accomplished in a typical 45-minute period. Any one of the tasks listed could easily take more than a traditional period, and teachers also need some time to reflect on their own. For these reasons, a block schedule, with its longer periods of time, is a better fit for this model. As the Chicago Public Schools discovered when they revamped professional development, they also needed a "shift in budget priorities"

FIGURE 5.2

Long-Range Inservice Planning

A Series of Four Half-Day Wednesday Plans

Wednesday 1: Announcements
        Good news
        Sharing
        Pressing Issues

        Curricular and instructional matters
            Teachers meet by discipline for 40 minutes—principal meets with each group.

        Student behavior issues
            Teachers meet by grade level for 40 minutes—principal meets with each group.

        Team planning/coordination
            Teachers meet by teams for 40 minutes—principal meets with each group.

Wednesday 2: Announcements
        Good News
        Sharing
        Pressing Issues

        Work on the year's theme (i.e., student-centered learning)
            Presentations by teachers on
                Defining student-centered learning
                What resources are available
                Demonstration lessons
                Individual planning for classroom implementation

Wednesday 3: Announcements
        Good News
        Sharing
        Pressing Issues

        Critique of first attempts at student-centered learning
            What worked? What did not work?
            What do you need?

        Sample lessons shared
        Real issues/problems shared

        Introduction of more resources

        Perhaps a quick presentation of some techniques

        Formation of pairs or triads for coaching as teachers continue to practice student-centered learning

Wednesday 4: Announcements
        Good News
        Sharing
        Pressing Issues

        Independent work on student-centered learning

(Russo, 2002, p. 1). Throughout this book, we are talking about fundamental shifts in the way we do business as public educators for the purpose of re-creating schools as places that attract and retain highly dedicated and talented professionals, who in turn provide high-quality education. Although I believe that resources in the current system can be reallocated, I also understand that the public, state government, and federal government will have to change the levels of funding for schools.

Each day, the core of the teams' planning time is dedicated to working together to coordinate instruction and share information. These are not complaint sessions, and each day's work needs to be accounted for in a team log. No schedule is perfect (some weeks will entail more parent meetings, and some weeks will include more conversations about specific students) but the general pattern outlined should be the norm, not the exception.

When I first attempted to create a system like this, I made several mistakes. First, I did not define the content of the session the day I visited the team. Immediately, the discussion moved to complaints about individual students, policies and procedures, and the like. Only when I mandated that my time with teams would consist of curricular discussion did such conversation happen. I actually refused to entertain questions or comments about procedure, discipline, and other such topics at this time. We could discuss those matters at other times, but these 20 or 30 minutes were devoted to educational, curricular, pedagogical matters.

The second error I made was not creating an accountability system for what happened in meetings. This is when the log began. In fact, I even provided a log sheet, which looked something like the one in Figure 5.3.

Using a log sheet meant that faculty always had a record of team activities that anyone could use as a reference. I also insisted that each day, each team post its meeting minutes for the rest of the school. By sharing this information, various teams could coordinate efforts or share information when appropriate. We were moving toward shifting our inservice focus away from a special event to a daily operation. Every day was an inservice day.

FIGURE 5.3
Team Meeting Log

Team: _____

Date: _____

Members present: _____

Curriculum planning: _____

_____

_____

_____

Parent contacts: _____

_____

Students discussed: _____

_____

_____

_____

Special education issues: _____

_____

_____

_____

Special projects/guests: _____

_____

At the Level of the Individual

Even this process was not focused tightly enough to create a fully operational professional development climate. You have to get down to the individual, supporting and celebrating his or her professional growth. Working in a school that had an evaluation cycle consisting of teachers' being evaluated once every three years, with the two intervening years being devoted to professional development activities, I developed the form in Figure 5.4.

This remarkably simple document became the basis for many very rich conversations about teaching and learning, as well as some fascinating projects. For instance, one music teacher and I negotiated an interesting process for his evaluation year. I would observe him conducting band class once. He would videotape himself running a rehearsal, and we would watch the tape together. At the teacher's request, I hired a music professor from a nearby university to shadow the band teacher for the day, discuss his work with him, and leave me a written report. Finally, the teacher wanted to create his own student feedback form and have me include the information in the year's summary evaluation. I was more than satisfied with the sources of information, and for the most part, the teacher himself was in control of the process. He had created his own professional growth or inservice learning and evaluation program for the year.

Teachers in supervision years created similarly creative contracts, without the final step of the summary evaluation. Some teachers kept journals, which I would read and respond to once each week. Others worked to implement new teaching techniques, keeping notes on their progress for our discussions. There was no limit to the possibilities other than the teacher's imagination, time, and space.

Nesting Goals

In the best of all possible worlds, a nesting process would occur, relating all of these levels of professional development to each other. Something in the teacher's individual goals should relate to something in the team's goals, which should relate to something in the school's goals. For instance, if the school's yearly theme is constructivist teaching, then each team should be spending some of its time developing constructivist lessons, and each teacher should be devoting some of his or her time to studying or implementing constructivism. This does not mean that there would not be other goals. There would. The teacher and supervisor would negotiate

---

FIGURE 5.4
Sample Goal-Setting Contract

Supervision/Evaluation Contract
Goal Setting

Date:

Name:

Cycle: Supervision I
        Supervision II
        Evaluation

Goals for the Year:

Professional Growth or Evaluation Activities:

Documentation:

This plan is a projected course of action for this school year. It may be changed by mutual consent of all parties involved.

_____   _____
Supervisor   Date

_____   _____
Teacher   Date

This plan has been successfully completed.

_____   _____
Supervisor   Date

these at the end of one year or the beginning of the next as part of the individual goal-setting process.

For this process to happen, the school has to have a professional development plan or theme, and we are back to the beginning: principals working with teacher committees to determine what is to be accomplished over the coming year. A sample plan appears in Figure 5.5.

In the next chapter, I will take a closer look at the role of goal setting, supervision, and evaluation in the retention of new teachers.

FIGURE 5.5

Sample Professional Development Plan

ABC County High School

School Professional Development Plan
2003–2004 School Year

1. Student Discipline
   a. Form a discipline committee representing all grade levels, consisting of teachers, paraprofessionals, parents, students, and administrators, not to exceed 12 people.
   b. The members of the committee research discipline models, visit other schools, attend workshops, and bring professional consultants into the school to observe and present their findings.
   c. The committee presents its conclusions to the full faculty with implementation plans.
   d. Implementation proceeds for the remainder of the year, with the committee overseeing training in the selected model and making adjustments to it in response to whatever issues arise.
   e. The committee will create some method of evaluation to illustrate what progress was made in this area.

2. Reading Across the Curriculum
   a. A cross-discipline committee of teachers will research current models of reading across the curriculum, visit other schools, attend conferences, and use consultants to gain as much knowledge as possible about this topic.
   b. The committee will determine a best course of action, presenting it to the full faculty for discussion.
   c. The committee will develop training modules, select or develop materials, and create an implementation plan.
   d. The committee will create a method to evaluate what progress was made in the area of reading across the curriculum.

Each teacher's goals must reflect, in some way, these two school themes in addition to whatever personal goals the teacher includes in his or her personal yearly plan.

For now, we can view evaluation and supervision as a subtopic within the general professional development program.

The Role of the Principal

The center of all the activity discussed in this chapter must be the principal. He or she will have to establish the systems and norms of a professional development school, creating a learning community. By example, and at first perhaps by mandate, he or she must embed the concept of professional growth as an integral part of the profession. All staff—teachers, administrators, paraprofessionals—will be required to work each year overtly at skill and knowledge improvement. The result—a dynamic, exciting, data- and research-driven climate—should appeal to those teachers who are looking for a professional experience with depth.

To retain the kind of people we want in education, we will have to create structures to maintain an exciting, growth-oriented professional atmosphere, thus satisfying the needs of individuals who desire intellectual challenge, growth, and accomplishment.

FIGURE 5.6

An Inservice Program Run by District Teachers and Administrators

DISTRICT 12 INSERVICE PROGRAM
JANUARY–MAY 2002

TEACHERS TEACHING TEACHERS

ARRANGED BY THE DISTRICT 12 INSERVICE COMMITTEE

3:30 p.m. sessions can have *unlimited enrollment*. 2:30 p.m. sessions are *limited to two participants* from each school, unless the appropriate principal allows a greater number. In all cases, participants must let Dan Heller know of their interest in attending *AT LEAST* one week prior to the session. Participants are responsible for arranging any necessary class coverage with their principals. Relicensure credit is available for these sessions.

January 15: Brain Gym

3:30 p.m.–4:30 p.m.

Brain Gym is a playful, active way for participants to experience the changes that are possible when using movement as a vehicle for learning enhancement. Brain Gym gives us conscious choice in learning so that "I can be in charge of how I feel" instead of "My reflexes and feelings are in charge of me."

January 29: Phonemic Awareness

2:30 p.m.–3:30 p.m.

Presentation will include techniques to engage children in listening for the sounds in words and manipulating the sounds by producing and replicating the phoneme, isolating the phoneme, phoneme segmentation, phoneme blending, rhyming, phoneme deletion, phoneme substitution, phoneme reversal, and Pig Latin through the use of sequential cumulative drills, puppet shows, and seasonal activities.

February 5: Brain-Based Teaching

3:30 p.m.–4:30 p.m.

Learn how the brain research of the last two decades informs best practices in teaching for understanding and memory.

February 12: Constructivism

2:30 p.m.–3:30 p.m.

Learn the meaning of this term and its implications for teaching and learning by actually participating in a constructivist lesson.

March 12: Learning Styles

3:30 p.m.–4:30 p.m.

Be introduced to the three learning styles and then decipher your own personal learning style. We will list ways children learn and brainstorm how to put this information into our daily lessons.

FIGURE 5.6 *continued*

An Inservice Program Run by District Teachers and Administrators

March 26: Taking Kids Outside—Teaching Sensory Activities

2:30 p.m.–3:30 p.m.

Learn useful techniques for teaching in the outdoors and also learn a variety of sensory activities/games that can be done inside or outside of the classroom. Best for teachers in grades K–6 but, with adaptation, can be used in any grade.

April 9: Teaching Narrative

3:30 p.m.–4:30 p.m.

This workshop will share ideas for teaching elementary students the basics of narrative. We will have a discussion on how to step through the writing process when students are writing narrative.

April 23: Burnout

2:30 p.m.–3:30 p.m.

When you just don't care any more. Early warning signs—counting the days until the next holiday—and what you can do about it.

May 7: Teaching Technology

3:30 p.m.–4:30 p.m.

Looking for ways to incorporate computers in your curriculum? In this introductory session you will be exposed to a range of activities that incorporate computers. Special attention will be given to the use of slide shows and Internet searches.

May 28: Using Multiple Intelligences to Learn the Continents and Oceans

2:30 p.m.–3:30 p.m.

This workshop will give teachers activities using the seven intelligences as a way for students to memorize the location of the oceans and continents. The activities have been used in the past with 2nd- through 4th-grade students.

6

Empowerment Through Individual Professional Growth

The professional atmosphere that will attract and keep excellent teachers is almost complete. The final piece is the ongoing individual professional growth of each staff member.

I remember being shocked when speaking with a psychiatric social worker who was employed in a large hospital. Her description of supervision went something like this: She would sit down with her supervisor and discuss her cases, how they were going, what she had done, and what other approaches might be available. This routine would happen on a regular basis. In fact, she told me that one of the features of a job a social worker looks for is the quality of the supervision the institution offers. I compared this to my own experience of having a supervisor walk into my classroom, take a bunch of notes, and then put a final document in my mailbox. The report often contained information about the room temperature, the neatness of the room, and also a few things about my teaching. Then and there I decided that professionals deserve professional supervision. If we hope to retain our best teachers, then we have to assure them that they will receive quality supervision supporting their professional growth.

Supervision Versus Evaluation

A thorny issue is the distinction between supervision and evaluation. Both are important, and they are closely related, but they are not the same thing. Whereas *supervision* is a process by which people assist each other's professional growth, *evaluation* is the means by which a professional is judged competent or not and thus impinges on whether the teacher gets a raise, retains the job, is put on probation, and the like (James, Heller, & Ellis, 1992, p. 98). Because both supervision and evaluation involve examining someone's work and doing something with the information gathered, many people have a difficult time distinguishing these terms. Sometimes, to help semantically, one can use the terms *formative evaluation* (supervision) and *summative evaluation* (evaluation).

The terms can be very volatile. I once spoke at a state teachers' convention on how teachers could supervise one another (peer supervision). However, I was not permitted to use the word *supervision* in the title of my session because of the reverberations of *administrator* it implied.

Trust, Knowledge, and Control

This matter of supervision and evaluation is a delicate one, exacerbated in our profession by the fact that the two roles are often played by the same person. Ideally, one should receive supervision from one person and evaluation from another. This scenario, however, is neither practical nor absolutely necessary if conditions are right. The three crucial factors that can make or break the supervision and evaluation process are trust, knowledge, and control.

The supervisor and supervisee must develop a strong sense of trust. The supervisor must have a deep knowledge of teaching and learning as well as adult development and adult education. The process should be, as much as possible, in the control of the supervisee; this approach removes much of the fear often associated with being observed. A principal can approach this control issue by having each teacher combine school-defined goals with personally defined goals, and by having teachers help define the process and evidence that will be used in the evaluation. The teacher's personal growth goals should fit into the school's overall professional development program. Sparks and Hirsh (1997) refer to this idea when they say, "This shift does not negate the value of teachers' perceptions regarding their needs, but rather places those needs within a larger context" (p. 14).

Control and Power

The issue of control leads to the question of power. Too often, people conceive of power as the ability to define the action of others. However, I would suggest, and have suggested, otherwise:

> So what is a useful definition of power? I propose that school personnel begin to see power as the ability to control oneself, not others. As teachers, we should empower students to take control of their lives. Similarly, schools must empower teachers to make decisions in their classrooms about what is best for their students. (Heller, 1994, p. 288)

Some form of teacher evaluation is a political given. Therefore, why not make it beneficial to the teacher and not just an exercise to provide information for employment status decisions? The more we can turn this process over to teachers, the more teaching will become a true profession. Within the larger context of institutional needs, teachers should have a substantial say in their own professional development and evaluation. One marker of a profession is the right of its members to police themselves. Teacher associations, then, should move away from their current labor union mentality that pits them against administrators and move toward the situation we have been developing in this book: teachers taking a large share in controlling entry into the profession, preparing the next generation of teachers, and maintaining the quality of the active teaching force.

Allowing teachers more control over their own professional lives has a ripple effect on the school. Sergiovanni and Starratt (1971) believe that teachers will withhold from students what is withheld from them. Therefore, oppressed teachers will be oppressive teachers. Glickman (1985) continues this thought with the observation that "teachers accept common goals for students and therefore complement each other's teaching, and when supervisors work with teachers in a manner consistent with the way teachers are expected to work with students, then—and only then—does the school reach its goals" (p. 4).

Glickman goes on to explain that when individual teacher goals are linked with institutional goals, the entire system works in harmony. He sees the supervision process as the glue that holds all such goals together, much as Sparks and Hirsh do. Goal setting with teachers, then, is at the heart of the supervisory process, and it is the first step in teachers exerting control over their individual professional development.

We can begin to give teachers control over their own professional destinies in the area of evaluation and supervision in three ways: by allowing them to develop some of their own professional goals, by giving them a larger voice in their individual evaluation, and by providing time for them to work with one another as peer supervisors. "Clever incentives may attract new teachers, but only improving the culture and working conditions of schools will keep them" (Johnson et al., 2001, p. 8).

Teacher Professional Goals

Establishing yearly goals with teachers is not a simple, mechanical task. Both teacher and supervisor should give the goal-setting process the attention and thought it deserves. I suggest that there be two or at most three goals. I would rather complete two excellent goals well than do a poor job with more. One of the goals should be explicitly related to institutional goals (e.g., the schoolwide project to incorporate more constructivist activities in the classrooms), and the other can be a more personal goal (e.g., the teacher's desire to expand his or her knowledge of young adult literature). In this way, even the school-related goal can be partially controlled by the teacher insofar as its specific form is concerned. What follows are two teacher goals, one a more institutionally oriented goal and the other a more personally oriented goal:

1. (Institutional orientation): To implement the Vermont Writing Portfolio Assessment program in 9th-grade classes.
2. (Personal orientation): To improve students' active engagement and decrease downtime in class by using improved time management skills.

Goals need to be specific and measurable. A good supervisor can help here. If a teacher suggests a goal such as "improved time management," then the supervisor might ask, "What would that look like? What would I see you doing? What would I see students doing, if you were successful with this goal?" Such questions force the teacher to define concretely what is to be accomplished. Furthermore, note that it is the teacher, not the supervisor, who does the defining. The supervisor may push for more specifics, but they are supplied by the teacher. The goal and its definition belong to the teacher. The supervisor is there to assist in the process, not to control it. Regarding the goals enumerated earlier, the supervisor would likely ask the teacher for a more detailed description of the portfolios, their contents, how they would be evaluated, and what would constitute success in an initial year of implementation. Clearly, the second goal begs for descriptors or indicators of success as illustrated previously. This defining process is not dissimilar to the way we approached writing a school mission statement earlier in the book. Abstract terms can be a useful place to start, but in the end everyone needs to be clear on what is supposed to happen. The supervisor and teacher can keep a record of these goals on a form like the one in Figure 6.1.

Note that in the form suggested here, the goals are not the only aspects of the process that are established in this first phase of professional supervision. What the teacher will do to accomplish the goals and how their accomplishment will be documented are also determined. Again, this specificity results in greater control and

FIGURE 6.1

Form for Establishing and Monitoring Yearly Professional Goals

Goal Setting Conference Record

Date: September 21, 2003

Name: Tim Jeffries

Cycle: Supervision
        Evaluation

Goals for the Year:

1. To implement the Vermont Writing Portfolio Assessment program in 9th-grade classes. This will result in each student having a writing portfolio that fulfills all the requirements of the State Portfolio System description and ensures that these portfolios will be scored according to the state system.

2. To improve students' active engagement and decrease downtime in class by using improved time management skills. Tim Jeffries will work with strategies such as lesson organization, material preparedness, sponge activities, overlapping, small-group work, and differentiated assignments to maximize students' on-task behavior and active involvement, thus wasting as little class time as possible.

Professional Growth or Evaluation Activities:

1. Tim will attend state writing network meetings and go through calibration sessions this year. He will assign an adequate number and range of writing assignments to allow each student to complete a portfolio by the end of the year. He will work with the state evaluation rubrics with his students all year and evaluate each final portfolio accordingly.

2. Tim and I will discuss various methods for maintaining student involvement and on-task behavior. I will also supply him with several readings on the subject. As Tim implements various techniques, he will keep notes on how well the strategies worked, which we will discuss together. We have defined *on-task behavior* as a student working on the current assignment. We have defined *active involvement* as a student doing something, such as writing, reading, or asking and answering questions, rather than simply sitting and listening.

Documentation:

1. Tim and I will meet once each quarter to discuss his work in both of the goal areas.

2. I will observe his classes at least twice to see how students are responding to the new time management strategies. Each observation will be followed by a postconference.

3. Tim and I will examine sample student portfolios together.

4. I will speak to his students about portfolios, to ascertain how much of the process they actually understand, especially the rubrics. Hopefully, I will be able to observe a writing portfolio lesson.

(continued on next page)

FIGURE 6.1 *continued*

Form for Establishing and Monitoring Yearly Professional Goals

5. We will examine a sample of the final portfolios and Tim's evaluation of them at the end of the year.

6. I will write a formal evaluation of Tim's work this year.

This plan is a projected course of action for this school year. It may be changed by mutual consent of all parties involved.

_____   _____
Supervisor   Date

_____   _____
Teacher   Date

This plan has been successfully completed.

_____   _____
Supervisor   Date

clarity of the teacher's professional growth activities, because these questions are answered collaboratively with the supervisor before the actual supervision or evaluation process begins. The teacher as professional is held accountable for his or her professional development, rather than having it forced upon him or her.

At the same time, a reduction in tension results from knowing what is going to happen in advance—no surprises. On the form, the choice of supervision or evaluation refers to a system in which teachers are evaluated once over a period of years, with nonevaluation years being purely professional growth or supervision years. Figure 6.2 offers an example of the prior form completed for a high school teacher in a supervision year.

Teachers' control of their professional development activities allows for the use of unique and interesting sources of information. A supervisor is not confined to the standard means of information

---

FIGURE 6.2

Goal Setting in a Supervision Year

Goal Setting Conference Record

Date: September 21, 2003

Name: Paul Dunn

Cycle: **Supervision**
     Evaluation

Goals for the Year:

Paul has two major goals for this year. The first is to experiment with offering college prep course materials to general-level students in anticipation of combining these two levels in future years. He is particularly interested in literature and vocabulary units. The second goal is to implement a new classroom management program, based on *Discipline with Dignity*, in all grade 10 classes.

Professional Growth or Evaluation Activities:

Paul will experiment with college prep materials, presenting them to general-level classes on several occasions, in preparation for our combining these two levels next year. He will keep notes on these lessons, which he and I will review for each unit attempted. He will invite me to observe at least one of these classes.

Documentation:

Paul will keep notes on his work with college prep materials in general-level classes. He will share these notes with me and invite me to observe at least one lesson.

I will be working with Paul on the classroom management program, observing classes, tracking discipline referrals, and tracking changes in student behavior.

This plan is a projected course of action for this school year. It may be changed by mutual consent of all parties involved.

_____   _____
Supervisor   Date

_____   _____
Teacher   Date

This plan has been successfully completed.

_____   _____
Supervisor   Date

gathering: observation, artifacts, comments that are in writing and signed. In my experience, teachers have suggested the following additional means of documentation:

- Journals
- Student feedback surveys
- Peer observation reports
- Lesson plans
- Annotated bibliographies
- Notes from outside professional observers
- Videotapes
- Audiotapes
- Personally created documents
- Photographs
- Copies of overheads and other presentation materials

When the teacher is in charge, anything agreed upon goes. As long as the teacher suggests and agrees to the method of information gathering, then that method can be used. This approach makes for a much fuller, more interesting, and comprehensive supervision process. Rich information fields yield rich professional conversation.

Trust

The crucial point here is trust. Acheson and Gall (1987) define trust as "the teacher's confidence that the supervisor has the teacher's interests at heart and that the supervisor will not use the data that emerge during supervision *against* the teacher" (p. 71). Without trust between the supervisor and the teacher, little of this creativity, risk taking, and professional adventure will take place.

Building trust is a long-term operation. However, all of the other parts of this book describe activities that will contribute to building trust, as teachers work with one another and with administrators in a system that values people trying new approaches and does not simply look for missteps to attack. Supervision as described here is a partnership between at least two people, not something that is done to one professional by another. The kind of supervision that I envision embodies the values of professionalism, self-determination, and the joy of discovery. It involves what Routman (2002) calls "ongoing professional dialogue to develop a reflective school community" (p. 32).

The process used for evaluation can be virtually identical to the one used here for supervision. Teachers still need to set goals, define those goals, and be part of the evaluation itself. A teacher will find the evaluation or supervision processes much friendlier if he or she has had some control over the process from the beginning. There should be no surprises.

Embedding Professional Development into the Day

The professional development model we seek is not an add-on; it is an integral part of the daily life of a professional. It creates the kind of atmosphere that will hold the most dynamic and exciting teachers in the profession. Sparks and Hirsh (1997) summarize the necessary transition for professional development in education as follows:

• From training conducted away from the job as the primary delivery system for staff development, to multiple forms of job-embedded learning.

• From an orientation toward the transmission of knowledge and skills to teachers by "experts," to the study by teachers of teaching and learning.

• From a focus on generic instructional skills, to a combination of generic and content-specific skills.

• From staff developers who function primarily as trainers, to those who provide consultation, planning, and facilitation services as well as training.

• From staff development provided by one or two departments, to staff development as a critical function and major responsibility performed by all administrators and teacher leaders.

• From staff development directed toward teachers as the primary recipients, to continuous improvement in performance for everyone who affects student learning.

- From staff development as a "frill" that can be cut during difficult financial times, to staff development as an indispensable process without which schools cannot hope to prepare young people for citizenship and productive employment (pp. 14–16).

An example of embedded professional development can be seen in the work of the Kellogg Middle School in Shoreline, Washington. The staff makes time during the school day six Fridays each year for teachers to get together in small groups of 6–10, when they develop professional development action plans that they then pursue together for two years (Hudson, 2002, pp. 76–77). Similarly, Sparks and Hirsh (1997) picture a system in which

> Teachers will develop their own expertise by spending an increasingly larger portion of their work day in various processes that will help them continually improve their understanding of the teaching and learning process. Teachers will regularly use action research, study groups, and the joint planning of lessons, among other processes, to refine their instructional knowledge and skills. (p. 14)

Professional development is where the excitement of teaching as a profession lives. This is where the best teachers thrive and want to be, applying new learning in their classrooms. This can be the teacher's equivalent of the scientist's laboratory, a place to try new ideas and discover fresh solutions to problems. A recent study by the National Commission on Teaching and America's Future concluded that the United States could cut teacher turnover by 50 percent by 2006. Among the factors noted by the researchers that would stem the tide of teachers leaving the profession were support in their professional lives and the existence of small, professional communities in which to work (Blair, 2003, p. 5). Both of these conditions could be enhanced in our schools by allowing teachers to work together, support one another, and become more involved in the lifeblood of the school: supervision, evaluation, and professional development.

In addition, teachers are completely capable of evaluating themselves as part of supervision or evaluation. This self-evaluation can lay the groundwork for rich professional dialogue between peers or teacher and evaluator. Saphier (1993) suggests that

> [i]t is also very productive to ask teachers to write a self-evaluation at some point in their cycle of professional growth. Administrators who do so ask for a written set of goal statements at the beginning of the year and a narrative in the spring from the teacher describing what was done and what progress was achieved. When administrators take these seriously, they signal that they do so by reading the self-evaluations carefully and having conferences with all teachers in turn about the written analysis. (p. 49)

Peer Teacher Supervision

One of the most empowering methods of supervision, in my experience, is to allow teachers to provide this service for one another. If indeed supervision is not summative evaluation, then why not allow those on the front lines, who are engaged in the same types of activities, to work with each other on a regular basis? Often, another teacher knows more about the day-to-day issues in the hallways or a particular curriculum than does an administrator. This knowledge is simply a function of proximity. In addition, two teachers may be teaching the same material, possibly making them more immediately familiar with it than their administrator. This practice has the further advantage of freeing additional time for the principal to work on the many other projects mentioned in previous chapters.

When you think of it, teacher peer supervision combines the best of several worlds: teacher empowerment, professional development, good supervision, and a sense of value. According to Acheson and Gall (1987), "the most available source of expertise is teachers themselves: to analyze their own teaching on the basis of objective data, to observe others' classrooms and record data teachers cannot record themselves, to help one another analyze these data and make decisions about alternative strategies" (p. 194).

Where this concept differs from others, such as teacher leaders or mentors, is that there is no difference in institutional level between the parties, and the process is voluntary. A first-year teacher has as much to say to a veteran as the experienced teacher has to the beginner. Issues of training and scheduling, however, must be addressed.

As a teacher, I was personally involved in the development and implementation of a peer teacher supervision program in a high school English department. That experience is summarized in *Peer Supervision: A Way of Professionalizing Teaching* (Heller, 1989). Eventually, teachers found the process so valuable that other departments in the high school and numerous elementary school teachers all became involved in the program.

As we have noted, one of the central factors in the supervision process is trust (Goldhammer, Anderson, & Krajewski, 1980, p. 26). To avoid compromising trust is very difficult when the supervisor is also your evaluator. If one is having trouble with classroom management, who is easier to approach for assistance, your evaluator or the teacher across the hall? When the role of supervisor is played by a peer, whose contract actually precludes him or her from evaluating others, this issue dissolves. Also, the peer supervision process is voluntary. One cannot mandate it, or its very spirit is destroyed. If the process takes hold and grows, a school atmosphere can develop into one of continuous professional growth. How wonderful for students to see teachers continually in each other's rooms, consulting and working together. The model of learning from one another is a powerful one, what the Critical Friends Group, a product of the National School Reform Faculty, calls a "reflective learning community . . . [of] friends who share a mission, offer strong support, and nurture a community of learners" (Bambino, 2002, p. 27). Critical Friends help teachers learn to build "collaboration and reflection among colleagues" (p. 25). The training of Critical Friends coaches focuses on "building the trust needed to engage in direct, honest, and productive conversations with colleagues about the complex art of teaching" (p. 25).

Of course, teachers will need some training in conducting preconferences, observations, and postconferences, modeled along the lines of clinical supervision. Excellent resources for these processes can be found in Goldhammer and colleagues (1980), Acheson and Gall (1987), Heller (1989), and Danielson (1996). For instance, Danielson tells us that a "framework for professional practice offers the profession a means of communicating about excellence. Educators have learned the value of a common vocabulary to describe teaching. . . . Such a framework is valuable for veterans as well as novices as they all strive to enhance their skills in this complex environment" (p. 5).

Can We Buy Some Time?

Another area of concern in peer supervision is time. One of the reasons for such a program in the first place is that most supervisors do not have the time for in-depth clinical supervision, which can take as many as five cycles of preconference, observation and postconference per teacher per year. Our schools are not designed to support a comprehensive system of supervision and evaluation. We will have to look at fundamental structural changes to the way we do business, as we have seen throughout this book. Although the program discussed here puts more people on the task, there remain the issues of schedules, time to meet, time to observe, and the like. Suggested here are several ways to work on these issues:

- *Form teams.* If three or four teachers decide to work together as peer supervisors, they can use their schedules creatively. For instance, Teacher A might have a prep period during which he or she could cover Teacher B's class, so that B could observe Teacher C. This system is less complex than it looks, and I have seen it work quite well.
- *Dedicate paraprofessionals to the program.* One or two paraprofessionals can open a great deal of time for teachers who want to work with one another. There would have to be a mechanism for signing up for the paras, but once that is done, the process is fairly simple. The paras can free teachers for observations, conferences, and even the time to analyze collected data. A paraprofessional is an expense, but so is the recruitment of new teachers.
- *Team teach.* Team teachers are in a unique position to observe one another. This approach can grow naturally out of the work situation.

- *Get creative.* Use journals that you and your peer pass back and forth. Videotape classes to "observe" at some other time. Share materials and ask how they worked. Recommend books to one another. Supervision does not have to be confined to observation.

Serious, Professional Conversations

This chapter has been about what Danielson (1996, p. 5) calls "serious, professional conversations." When we can create an atmosphere in which people are excited to talk about teaching and learning, when individual teachers feel that their ideas and personal goals are honored, I believe that we have established the last major component that makes a school climate attractive to professionals and encourages them to stay. Danielson describes this atmosphere as one that educators create.

> It is through serious, professional conversations about the components comprising the framework [for teaching] that the components are validated for any particular setting. As educators study the components and consider them within individual contexts, they can determine which components and elements are applicable and which are not. This process is critical to both enriching the professional lives of educators and to ensuring that the components used in a given setting actually do apply there. Only educators in that setting can make those determinations. (p. 5)

We now find ourselves at an interesting point: a description of the principal who will make all this happen. Who is this remarkable person? Can anybody really do all this? Indeed, it will take extraordinary principals to not only stem the tide of the teacher shortage but also bring our schools out of the past and into a professional future.

7

A Challenging Role
for the Principal

Who is this amazing person who will restructure education to attract and retain new talent? How will he or she build program partnerships with local colleges, develop school inservice plans, work with individual teacher goals, hire personnel, conduct formal evaluations, ensure that the induction system is operational, promote the institutional philosophy, keep order, conduct meetings, work with boards and communities, maintain the building, take care of teachers with personal problems, be a friend to all, be a boss to all, write budgets, oversee curriculum, eat lunch with the kids, and oversee pedagogy? Who? For me, the answer is simple: There is no such person. *A New York Times* article describes the job of principal as follows:

> [T]he job has always been far less colorful than Hollywood would lead us to believe. And it has never been harder on the people in it, a circumstance that helps explain a national shortage that has left some states struggling to find a permanent principal for one of every five schools. (Steinberg, 2003, p. 1)

This could be the start of another book about educational personnel shortages, but that topic is for another time.

Certainly, fantastic principals and schools do exist. There are blue ribbon schools, lab schools, and schools that turn around ghetto populations. Yet, the logical conclusion to everything I have said so far points to the need to make teaching into a profession, which means sharing power, responsibility, and tasks. Throughout the previous chapters, we have developed a vision of teachers taking on the roles that other professionals do, such as having control over their own growth and decisions, helping train the next generation, having some say in gatekeeping, sharing knowledge with one another, and generally being seen as people who do a great deal more than simply deliver information to children. The overwhelming list of tasks cataloged in the first paragraph needs to be shared among the members of the teaching staff, thus solving two issues. First, the tasks finally all get done. Second, teachers take on much more of a professional role, specializing in various tasks and moving along a career ladder based on talent, not years of service.

Does this sharing reduce the role of the principal? It does not. In fact, the role becomes more important and complex than ever. First, however, the principal has to be comfortable enough with him- or herself, and have sufficient ego strength, to be able to let go. According to Lambert (1998), "leadership requires the redistribution of power and authority. Shared learning, purpose, action, and responsibility demand the realignment of power and authority. Districts and principals need to explicitly release authority, and staff need to learn how to enhance personal power and informal authority" (p. 9).

Lambert goes on to explain why the principal's role is not diminished as a result of this dispersal of authority and responsibility:

> The work [of the principal] is much more complex than we thought it was; it demands a more sophisticated set of skills and understandings than ever before. It is more difficult to build leadership capacity among colleagues than to tell colleagues what to do. It is more difficult to be full partners with other adults engaged in hard work than to evaluate and supervise subordinates. (p. 24)

The job does get smaller, but it does change. The principal will become the chief adult educator in the building, helping develop the necessary staff skills to make the transition to the ideal professional situation possible. If the principal models a willingness to take risks, other parties will have to take risks for the greater good as well. One group that comes to mind is the teacher association, which often looks upon change with a suspicious eye.

Teacher Associations

I am always saddened when I encounter groups claiming to be educational associations that are, in fact, labor unions. There is nothing wrong with labor unions, but they are not professional associations—another example of one entity trying to wear two hats. It is unfortunate that teachers need the protection of contracts and labor unions. They should be revered as those who nurture and prepare our children to take their places in the next generation of society's leaders. Instead, unions have developed to offer teachers protection from arbitrary decisions about their jobs that may result from boards whose members are constantly changing with yearly elections, individual personality disputes, and power being placed in the hands of people not well versed in the profession itself. Because the educational structures in the United States tend to be unprofessional in the ways we have been discussing here, it is natural that society does not treat teachers as professionals. Why do we have lay boards to tell highly trained and experienced individuals how to do their jobs, what to buy, what programs are necessary? In this way the system infantilizes teachers and administrators, and even superintendents. In contrast, a hospital board may decide on whether to build a new wing or what to do with incidents of sexual harassment, but it does not tell the surgeon where to make the incision.

School Boards, Trust, and Professionalism

School boards will have to let go, taking the risk of trusting the employees they have hired to do their jobs well. At times I have thought that some school boards could save a great deal of money if they simply fired all the administrators, because they wanted to run everything themselves anyway. They could then hire much less expensive people whose job would be simply to carry out their decisions and orders. The whole operation is inside out and upside down. When are we going to allow educators to educate, based on their training, experience, and collective wisdom, while insisting that boards limit their work to policy decisions and overall maintenance of the system?

Perhaps this will happen more easily once teachers' associations stop shielding their weakest members and share in the task of policing their own ranks. People trust professionals, but they indicate a tremendous lack of trust in many school systems. We may seek a second opinion, but then we allow the doctor to do his work. Do we tell the lawyer what the law is, or do we ask? We take our car to the mechanic, tell her what is going on, and then let her figure out what is causing the problem. We don't stand there and tell her which wrench to use. Why is it so difficult for people to accept the idea that teachers may know more about what they are doing than the general public does?

Teachers do indeed need protection from arbitrary employment decisions, but they also need to take a much greater part in the collective control of the quality of their ranks. I mean this in a less threatening way than it may sound. If we really were able to construct the system described in this book, with the extensive training, support system, and ongoing evaluation procedures we have considered, then we could accomplish our goal by extending the probationary period for teachers to at least five years. By that time, and with all the help offered, one should be able to determine by consensus of all parties involved whether a teacher is right for the position. This probationary period seems to make sense. As Wise (2003) points out, "how is it. . . that a substantial period of apprenticeship is required for those who trim our nails, our curls, or even the limbs of our trees, but it is not required for those who are to help shape the minds of the next generation?" (p. 56).

An Interesting History

I suspect that the problems of professionalism and protection lie in the history of our schools and their relationship to society. Without going into detail, I will simply say, first, that U.S. schools grew up as the province of women, when women were not much respected in the work force. Second, everyone has gone to school, so everyone knows all about schools. People believe that this experience makes them experts. They went to school, they are now successful, so why should anything change? There is a logic to this perspective, but the argument disregards all the changes in the world over the last 25 years of those particular adults' lives. Finally, because schools deal with our most precious members of society, our children, parents tend to pay close attention to what schools are doing.

Keeper of the Vision

Many aspects of the world of teaching need to change if principals are to lead in the direction of the ideal school situation I have been describing. While the principal does have a part to play in all the tasks listed in the first paragraph of this chapter, I believe that the job can be reduced to one primary role: keeper of the vision. The principal should always be checking what is happening against the school's vision or mission. Does this new program fit the school's definition of respect? Is it student centered? According to Patterson (1993), "leading is defined as *the process of influencing others to achieve mutually agreed upon purposes for the organization.* . . . In other words, the organization's goals are supported by all people involved, and these people in turn support those who are, at that particular time, leading them toward the goals" (p. 3).

The principal is the hub that holds everything together. Continuing this image of a wheel, each spoke represents a program, teacher, and committee of the school, and the spinning outer rim is the running school, the process of teaching and learning in a professional atmosphere. Someone has to check and maintain the integrity of the parts, making sure that all runs according to plan.

Making sure that all runs according to plan is not the same as running everything according to plan. Thus, another change emerges. Patterson (1993) suggests that enlightened leaders "turn their back on the value of exercising personal authority over events and people to get the right decisions made and, instead, embrace the idea of overseeing the development and implementation of a set of core values that will drive decision making by all employees" (p. 5).

The system will have to afford teachers much more autonomy, respect, and accountability as we change how our schools look, feel, and operate. Patterson (1993) includes five core values needed for this new type of school to work: openness to participation, openness to diversity, openness to conflict, openness to reflection, and openness to mistakes. The principal is a checkpoint. He or she watches to ensure that the school is evolving in the desired direction. If it is not, the principal will question what is happening, helping redirect the activity or change the vision to match what has become the newly accepted direction. According to Patterson, "leaders create an environment of safety, so all employees can freely express their thoughts without fear of recrimination" (p. 11).

Thoughts are one thing, actions another. Of course, no true debate can occur in a closed atmosphere, but once a decision is made, once a vision is accepted, everyone in the organization expects follow-through. In this respect, I believe that the new principal should have a far greater say in the future employment of each teacher than he or she does now. Although teachers do need protection from arbitrary decisions, an administrator should be allowed to make a convincing case for dismissal or disciplinary action without having to resort to three years of a paper trail, long hearings with lawyers, and seemingly endless obstacles. Teacher associations should be partners with administrators in guaranteeing that the professional forces of any school are excellent, both as teachers and as members of the professional organization.

Nothing New Under the Sun

What I find most interesting about my readings in the "new" leadership is that these ideas have existed for quite some time. The Chinese Taoist Lao-tzu probably lived some time around the fifth or sixth century B.C.E. His work, the *Tao Te Ching* or *The Book of the*

Way, contains the core of Taoist wisdom. Chapter 17 reads as follows (replace the word *master* with *principal* or *leader*):

> When the Master governs, the people
> are hardly aware that he exists.
> Next best is a leader who is loved.
> Next, one who is feared.
> The worst is one who is despised.
>
> If you don't trust people,
> you make them untrustworthy.
>
> The Master doesn't talk, he acts.
> When his work is done,
> the people say, "Amazing:
> we did it, all by ourselves!" (Lao-tzu, 1988, p. 17)

The leader must not only create an atmosphere in which this process can happen but also develop the skills in members of the organization to make this atmosphere possible. In a sense, the successful transformational principal will become egoless. He or she will be a force to create an environment of professionalism, providing the skills, means, and atmosphere for this outcome to occur. If the principal gets tripped up by his or her own ego, wanting things to go one way rather than being open to all ideas and the sharing of power, authority, and responsibility, we will be caught once again in the old mold of paternalistic/maternalistic control. The goals have to be wider than the individual, expanding to encompass what is best for the vitality and success of the teaching and learning process as it applies to everyone in the educational community, particularly the students.

Professionalism, Power, Autonomy . . . Responsibility

As the job of teacher becomes more professional, the teacher should be held to ever-higher levels of accountability. For instance, when

I first used to hire teachers, I always worked with a committee of teachers as part of the process, from résumé reviews, to the interviews, to the final selection. However, I reserved veto power, because after we all walked away from the table, I was going to be held accountable for the choice. None of the others would ever have to answer for the quality of the new teacher. Therefore, if I thought that a candidate was a person I could not work with, then I could not allow that candidacy to go forward. However, if I was not the only person ultimately to be held accountable because we had an induction program, a mentoring program, and a chance to look at the individual in preservice programs, then the picture would change. In that case, a bad hire would reflect something askew in the program. Many of us would have to get together to figure out what went wrong, and this only after all of our methods of teacher assistance had been exhausted.

This issue of responsibility has plagued reform efforts, because those efforts are too often ahead of political and legal realities. Hallinger and Hausman studied this issue as part of their examination of the principal's role in restructured schools. They saw this as particularly problematic in shared decision making. "Under school-based management, the School Leadership Council has become the locus of educational decision making. The question of who is accountable for decisions reached by group consensus under school-based management, however, remains unclear" (Hallinger & Hausman, as cited in Murphy & Louis, 1994, p. 164).

Patterson (1993) has an interesting point of view on this issue. He asks the question of what level of accountability people want to assume. If groups want to take part in the decision-making process but do not want responsibility, then, according to Patterson, they are opting for shared decision making. "In shared decision making, everybody contributes to the process of decision making, but only one person [the principal] is held accountable for the decision" (p. 61). He then concludes that a principal will inevitably have to retain veto power if he or she simply cannot defend the group's decision. However, he tempers this view by saying that if participants have been adequately trained in consensus-building methods, and if the atmosphere is the open one I have been describing, then the group should be able to make 95 percent of its decisions by consensus and without the use of the veto. Otherwise, performance accountability must be directly connected to the responsibility for making decisions.

Principal as Public Relations Expert

The principal is the institution's face, representing the decisions and directions the school chooses to pursue. He or she speaks to the public and the board for the school. The principal is the lead representative in contacts with other organizations such as service groups, schools, local businesses, and government officials. This is not to say that teachers do not also represent the school or meet outside groups. However, the principal is the primary liaison between the school and the surrounding community. He or she is the keeper of the vision and therefore represents that vision before the many public entities that have an interest in our children's education.

Technical skills are great to have, but the principal does not have the time to employ many of them. Consider, for instance, building a master schedule. This task should be the job of a computer expert or perhaps an assistant principal. The principal should be able to explain what the schedule is supposed to accomplish (the vision) but then leave the job of implementing that vision to someone else who has the necessary knowledge and skills to make the vision a reality. Aren't the countless hours necessary to build a schedule in a large school really a waste of time for the principal? The job itself is not a waste of time; in fact, it is of extreme importance. But it is not the job of the principal, who is too busy keeping the vision.

We could go through the same argument for discipline, the physical plant, bus schedules, food service, and the like. Does a CEO hire custodians? Does she evaluate the people who work in the building cafeteria? No. However, the CEO does set the tone, meet the public, set direction, coordinate with other institutions, and watch the operation for trouble spots. This is my principal. The most important skill this principal has is communication. I do not believe that a president of the United States makes many decisions alone. He is surrounded by a bevy of diverse experts who explain to him the many technical aspects of a situation that no one person could possibly know. After all, we have had presidents with no military background whatsoever, yet they were nonetheless commanders in chief of the country's entire armed forces.

What the president does have to do, however, is communicate decisions to the people of the nation. Now, I do not want to push this analogy too far. I understand the mistrust many have for government, the suspicion of secrets, and the existence of classified information. The point is that the principal is a communicator, an embodiment of the school, and a diplomat. He or she is also a jack of all trades, but, as I have suggested, his or her energy should not be taken up with many of the daily operations that currently often fall to the principal. As we rethink the profession, we must rethink its administrative structure as part of that reconceptualization.

Principals Build Capacity for Leadership and Decision Making

Lambert (1998) sees two critical conditions necessary for a school to be able to build leadership capacity throughout its staff. First, "the school would need a significant number of skillful teacher-leaders who understand the shared vision of the school and the full scope of the work underway, and who are able to carry them out. These teachers ideally would be involved in the selection and induction of the new principal." Second, "school staff would need to be committed to the central work of self-renewing schools. This work involves reflection, inquiry, conversations and focused action—professional behaviors that are an integral part of daily work" (pp. 3–4).

Lambert goes on to explain that principals are largely responsible for building leadership capacity. This role can be served by turning staff questions back onto the staff ("What do you think?"), enjoining staff to think through issues together with the principal, explicitly talking through everyone's roles at staff meetings, and so forth. The principal cannot allow staff to use the excuse of seeing the solution to important issues as "the principal's job." Instead, he or she will have to work to create an atmosphere of general ownership, empowerment, and leadership. Only in this way will most, if not all, teachers take responsibility for the successful operation of the school. The principal must consistently put forth the institutional philosophy, making it very public (Lambert, 1998).

Rosenblum, Louis, and Rossmiller (1994) state the following about good leadership:

> Good leadership [is] considered to be one that facilitates collaboration, communication, feedback, influence, and professionalism in the following ways:
> - By providing leadership through establishment of a vision and value system.
> - By having consistent policies to delegate and empower others, thus sharing leadership.
> - By modeling risk taking.
> - By focusing on people, nurturing staff members, and helping them to grow.
> - By emphasizing the educational aspects of the school rather than the purely technical aspects of the school. (p. 120)

The principal can no longer be the traditional boss, telling people what to do and supposedly having all the answers. Leadership becomes a collective issue, with the principal being sure to provide training for the faculty that will allow them to take on many of the traditional roles of leadership. The principal's role moves from that of a fixer to that of an empowerer (Glickman, Allen, & Lunsford, 1994, p. 208). In Murphy and Louis's (1994) conclusion to a review of research studies of leadership in transformational schools, they state that "the researchers in this volume document how principals manage complexity by diffusing it into the organization. Principals in these cases reject—at least intellectually—the notions that they must know everything, solve every problem, and be all things to all people all the time" (p. 271).

Making the Job Doable

The idea is not to make the principal's job easier but to make it different and doable. In its present iteration, what too often happens is that certain tasks simply do not get done. Problems with buses, snow plows, and discipline do not wait. One must attend to them as they occur. One can always put off that classroom observation, that meeting with the new teachers, that appearance at the student council meeting. The particulars of the day can consume the principal with activities that are important but not important enough to supplant other activities, and certainly not the tasks that the principal should spend substantial time on. At some level, everything can eventually get to the principal's desk, but the principal does not always have to be the key player in every issue. Joel I. Klein, New York City's school chancellor, acknowledged this problem when he moved to give principals the authority to hire their own assistants, thus freeing themselves from excessive paperwork (Goodnough, 2002).

Rosenblum and colleagues studied what they call "Teacher Quality of Work Life" in schools that were shifting their way of doing business, or restructuring. These schools ran into the difficulty we have been discussing: the conflict of trying to manage an institution and be an educational leader at the same time. They found successful principals understood the importance of the managerial function but dealt with it by delegating much of the task to others.

> But by delegating these tasks—often to assistant principals (APs)—they were able to budget a substantial amount of time for instructional leadership activities. . . . It appears that it was the APs who were carrying out the technical managerial functions to keep the school running, which freed up the principal for educational and visionary leadership. (Rosenblum et al., 1994, p. 111)

As I have been arguing throughout this book, we must find ways to strip the principal's role of as many managerial functions as possible, even if this means hiring a separate school manager, to create the time needed for the principal to provide educational leadership, train in consensus building, and keep the vision while supporting the building of professional institutions of education.

Support for Change in the Principal's Job

The situation among principals is not that different in some respects from that of teachers, and similar remedies to what I have proposed for teachers are beginning to be put into place for administrators. For instance, 48 percent of Washington, D.C.'s, principals are of retirement age (Moreno, 2003, p. 2), and New York City has more than 225 interim principals because of a lack of high-quality applicants (Goodnough, 2002, p. 1). As in the case of teachers, this situation may also present an opportunity to change the system, if turnover is large enough.

In response to this issue, a new program for developing principals now exists in New York City, Chicago, San Francisco, and Washington, D.C. The new training involves a summer institute, followed by a fellowship, during which the aspiring principal spends one full year working with a mentor principal, helping run a school. This is followed by a two- to three-year residency program. Individuals who are in the fellowship part of the training will be paid at the level of assistant principal (Moreno, 2003, pp. 1–2). This program sounds remarkably like what I have been suggesting for teachers. Now is the time to initiate real school reform, not patchwork reform. This is also a call to institutions of higher education to adjust their principal licensing programs to reflect the world we are in, not the one that existed when the programs were designed.

We have applied patches to our public school system for so long now that I sometimes wonder whether anything is underneath them or whether the patches themselves have become the fabric of public education. Many of the innovations I have suggested so far can be done, but I would hate to see them done as patches. Yet, to implement all of them requires a fundamental rethinking of public education, not adding more patches. Once again, a teacher shortage and a principal shortage may be the opening needed to rebuild the system, not simply repair it.

Evolution of Schools and Roles

Certainly, all of the necessary changes described here cannot be accomplished at once. A school will need to have a plan that includes a sequence of programs to be researched, developed, and implemented. To do this, the school must collect the right people for the job. Again, we can turn to the teacher shortage as the opportunity to make this happen. New roles and responsibilities will be the order of the day.

However, I encourage evolution, not revolution. Revolution can often represent the explosion of pent-up energy. To evolve, on the other hand, means to change fundamentally and incrementally from the inside out. The evolved school is one that has followed a long path of systematic and deep transition to something new. These kinds of changes are part of the fabric of the institution, not merely the result of a sudden, explosive transfer of power. This change process, like so much else, will be largely in the principal's hands.

This chapter has been the most difficult to write, because it makes so many assumptions about and demands on the many groups who hold an interest in our schools. I have to remind myself and the reader that this book is a "what-to" and not a "how-to" book. In other words, I am trying to create a vision of what should be, but I, too, do not have all the answers regarding implementation of this vision. To create the schools described here, principals, teachers, school boards, parents, government, unions, and teacher/principal preparation institutions will have to collaborate at unprecedented levels.

The principal will certainly be at the center of this transition. He or she is going to need a lot of help and a lot of room. People will have to accept mistakes as part of the process rather than pouncing on them as reasons to declare failure. Power will have to be distributed from traditional control loci to new ones. Paradoxically, this process leads to more power for everyone. Roles have to be clarified and understood. Risk, trust, support, caring, honesty, and humility are crucial human characteristics in this process, without which, I fear, the dream will die.

For me, the final question is: do we have the political, intellectual, and personal will to see such a change through to the end, even if it takes several generations to complete, causes discomfort and even pain, and challenges us to rethink innumerable assumptions and habits of tradition? I believe that we can do it.

Restructuring the Profession

To summarize my thesis is simple. There is a teacher shortage because the conditions under which teachers work too often drive employees away. Darling-Hammond (2003) sees the challenge as follows: "The problem does not lie in the numbers of teachers available; we produce many more qualified teachers than we hire. The hard part is keeping the teachers we prepare" (p. 7).

If we want the very best and brightest to work with our children, then we have to appreciate them, trust them, empower them, and treat them as professionals with specialized skills and knowledge. What I am suggesting here is a careful, deliberate rethinking and restructuring of public education in the United States. Such an approach will entail sharing power, providing better training, giving up some traditional assumptions and values, and expressing enormous trust. How else are we going to reverse the trend that began in the 1990s (Darling-Hammond, 2003) of more teachers leaving the profession than are entering it?

The Art of War

I do not see the value in revolution. Revolutions leave too much damage in their wakes. Rather, I would like to see a concerted effort to move education along an evolutionary path that results in the vision I have developed in the previous chapters. Then I think we will see not only enormous improvements in our educational system but also the end of the teacher shortage. We would do well to heed the advice of Sun Tzu, who wrote *The Art of War* about 2,300 years ago in China:

> And so one skilled at employing the military
> Subdues the other's military but does not do battle,
> Uproots the other's walled city but does not attack,
> Destroys the other's state but does not prolong.
> One must take it whole when contending for all-under-heaven.
> Thus the military is not blunted and advantage can be whole.
> This is the method of strategy of attack. (Sun Tzu, 2001, p. 10)

Change without battle—systematic and complete change, well paced but not hasty change—is the goal recommended by Sun Tzu if we apply his "battle" to our changes in education.

An Ironic Economy

At this moment, a weakened economy gives the illusion that the teacher shortage is abating. Educators are being let go all over this country. That does not alter my argument. At some point, the economy will turn around, and then we will find ourselves in the same spot we are in today. Once more, we may see the current economic situation as a possible advantage. Moving the system may be easier if it is a smaller system overall. Now is the time to set new precedents, new distributions of power, new roles and responsibilities, and new attitudes.

We Can Do It; We Can Win

Later in *The Art of War*, Sun Tzu (2001) recommends:

> If it is not advantageous, do not act.
> If it is not attainable, do not employ troops.
> If it is not in danger, do not do battle. (p. 56)

The recommendations I have made are advantageous. They should improve teacher preparation and reduce recruitment costs. They should make schools more professional, exciting, dynamic places of learning and growth for everyone. Although I have not emphasized the point, everything in this book, while intended to staunch the personnel leak in the profession, ultimately leads to an improvement in teaching and learning. All change should, at its base, improve services for students. This is the first argument for action.

Are these changes attainable? I believe that they are. I know I have written some negative remarks about educational associations and school boards. I also know that many educational associations and school board members do not fit those negative descriptions. These are the people we need to mobilize. My experience is limited, because I have not worked all over the United States. I have traveled enough, however, to allow me to have spoken to teachers from almost every state, and the frustrations I hear are often remarkably similar. I have also cited numerous examples of schools and systems that are making the necessary changes, that are transforming into the professional institutions we so desperately need. A teacher shortage means more teachers hired at the lower end of the salary scale. This scenario translates into savings that can be used for professional development. Greater numbers of retired teachers place a rich resource of expertise at our fingertips. More stable faculties mean fewer dollars spent in recruitment efforts such as advertising and signing bonuses. The need for new staff means the opportunity to hire the people who are willing to engage in the journey of transformation and who have the skills to make the journey successful. Thus, we should "employ the troops" to attain this victory.

Without trying to sound too dramatic, I think we can say that we are in danger. Our educational system is crying for reform, yet the natural inclination of humans is to resist change, holding onto what is comfortable. Comfort can mean complacency, and complacency can mean that the fire has gone out. We have more students than ever before and more problems at our doors than in the past. Every child is entitled to a free and appropriate education. This mandate is probably the single most difficult one ever handed to the public education system. To meet it, we need to convert our schools into vibrant, problem-solving institutions that welcome challenge rather than avoid it. This transformation, too, will require a stable, committed, and highly professional staff. All of Sun Tzu's admonitions for action have been met. Now is the time to act.

Who Should Set the Agenda for Change?

There is a barrier to action, most recently exemplified by the No Child Left Behind Act. Although this act is unquestionably well intentioned, once again we see people who are noneducators, far removed from the actual day-to-day activity of schools, deciding for us what we should do and how we should do it. I can only assume that the basis for the locus of control residing outside the schools themselves is a general lack of trust. If the system I have described actually existed, then perhaps the public would have more confidence in schools. When I consider the complexity of this legislation, layered on top of enormously complicated special education laws and the daily challenges of handling discipline matters, addressing social issues, and engaging wandering minds, I have to wonder where we are going and whether we will ever get there.

I have often speculated on what might happen if the many restrictions on education were lifted. What if the public simply told us what it wanted students to be able to do and know by the end of their years in school, and then left the rest to us? I can accept a society having a lot to say about the goals for its children. After that, however, why not leave the rest to the professionals in the field? Obviously, people do not currently consider schools up to the task, and in some ways they may be right. Unlike the preparation received by other professionals, the current system of teacher preparation, according to Arthur E. Wise, president of the National Council for Accreditation of Teacher Education, is inadequate to live up to the public's expectations.

> The [teacher] certification process is weak in comparison to the licensing process in most professions. The public should expect the certification process to provide independent validation of teaching candidates' liberal arts education, content knowledge, teaching knowledge and skill, and teaching performance. Most state certification processes fall short of that expectation. (2003, pp. 56, 42)

Once again we can look at the medical profession for a model. Certainly doctors must meet rigorous standards of training, ethics, and practice. Nonetheless, the goal that society has defined for physicians is basically to provide good care and bring people back to health. Doctors do not have to reach a 100 percent cure rate in 12 years. They also have the privilege of choosing their own approach to a clinical issue, and patients can seek second opinions and decide what they think is the best course of action.

Similarly, if schools were dynamic, problem-solving institutions, then the goal would be to help each student meet whatever standards had been set by whatever methodology was deemed appropriate by the staff. If parents did not like what the school wanted to do, then they could always seek education elsewhere (a second opinion). Time would also become less of a factor. I have never met an educator who did not agree that every child learns differently and at a different rate. Why, then, don't we work with students until they are done, not until the year ends? There would be no issue of social promotion if each student progressed at his or her own rate. The job of the school would be to bring the student to the point of meeting all standards or to explain why this could not be done or why it might take more or less time than the average student would need. Does the doctor have only 10 months to cure the patient regardless of the patient's condition, environment, life habits, and other variables?

Obviously, I am arguing for an extensive redesign of the public education delivery system. In my opinion, this redesign is ultimately what is needed to make education a profession that attracts and retains excellent personnel. Anything less is unacceptable for a structure that is charged with the care and education of our children.

I wrote in the previous chapter that this book is about what to do, not how to do it. Many resources, too numerous to list here, are available that consider all the aspects of education I have discussed, with examples of schools that have made the changes. This is not something done quickly. Changes of this number and magnitude will be part of multiyear plans. I believe that this vision can be realized if we have the political will to make it happen.

Roles and Responsibilities

All the key players—government, boards, parents, teachers, unions, administrators, students, and communities—have to trust one another and take the plunge. The center has to be the student's welfare, not power, career, control, or regulation. Once we commit to the process, we can begin to effect the necessary changes to improve the system. The teacher shortage, as I see it, is merely a symptom of a much larger and more fundamental issue: the need to restructure education into a profession like other professions. Old assumptions will have to give way, as will old methods of teacher preparation, hiring, evaluation, and dismissal. If all the players do not accord each other the respect they deserve, if we do not finally face the issue of regulating the quality of teaching professionals, and if we do not clearly define the roles and responsibilities of each layer of the system, then I see little chance of reaching our full potential.

There is a difficult cycle to break here. Communities may not trust schools because of the low standards for teacher licensure, the difficulty encountered in trying to remove the unqualified, and a mountain of vested interest and resistance to change. How can we expect communities to treat educators like professionals when we do not yet have the system to make education a profession? I think the first move belongs to the schools. We need to win the faith of our consumers by acting as professionals. That means no more talking about students openly in the faculty room, no more failing to keep up with the professional literature, and the like. We have to make the leap, by our actions, our attitudes, and our values. Then we may begin to reverse the lack of trust in our schools.

Get the Stars Out of Your Eyes

I suspect that many people will read this book and see me as an anti-teacher idealist with respect to how I wish to see educators treated. However, remember that I have no tolerance for teachers being treated unprofessionally or as if their knowledge and training were useless. At the same time, however, I have no tolerance for mediocre performance in educators. I have no tolerance for disrespect between any parties. I have no use for people who speak the language of collaboration but ultimately cannot let go of power and control. There is no place for arrogance, there is no place for protecting those who are not sufficiently skilled, and there is no place for grandstanding in education. Education is hard work that demands of educators high levels of skill and training. Our schools should be preparing their own human resources, making sure that only the most qualified individuals are attracted and retained by the profession. Once again, this process takes time. People are not necessarily natural consensus builders, but they can learn. They may not have all the skills to deal with some difficult students, but they can acquire methods through study and practice.

If the political will is there, then we can prevail. We must organize budget overrides, help communities understand the importance of professional development, work with institutions of higher learning, and take action to help elect the best possible school board members.

Starry Eyes Are the Result of Real Experience

I have been involved with many initiatives like the ones I have discussed here, such as professional development schools, induction programs, shared governance, preservice programs, peer supervision, general professional supervision, and professional development. All of these innovations have been tried successfully, but not, to my knowledge, all in one school. Some school district or individual school must take the bit to see what happens. Of course, we will falter, hesitate, fail, and start again. That persistence is ultimately how to make progress. We cannot allow ourselves or our communities to be scared away by one false start or unsuccessful new program.

Each time I have been involved in one of these restructuring or change efforts, all sorts of obstacles stood in the way. Much of this book flows from my own experience and frustrations with the many roadblocks I have encountered during my 28 years in education. The ostensible topic of the discussion has been the teacher shortage. As I reflected on this phenomenon, the first question I asked was "Why?" This question led me to see the many factors in educational systems that can drive teachers away or fail to attract good people in the first place.

Layer after layer began to fold back as I read extensively on the shortage issue. Clearly, many of those frustrating obstacles that I have run into are intimately related to the failure of education to become a professional endeavor. I can imagine some readers asking at this point why I am still working as an educator after the way I have criticized the system so thoroughly. The reason is that I love it. I love it because of the potential I see for something better and the belief that the job can be done.

Each time a teacher thanked me for writing a thoughtful and useful classroom observation report, I would get a glimpse of the vision. When a student's eyes lit up with understanding or when a student came to say "thank you" 10 years after graduation, I was inspired to keep on going. Working with teacher-interns, listening to their problems, helping them find solutions, and seeing their growth made me feel that I was giving something back to the field. And I was not hesitant to suggest that some of these interns not become teachers. I have also counseled out teachers whom I have hired, once I saw that they did not have the skills necessary for success. More of them might have made it if we had had some of the support systems I have described.

Being a guest teacher in classrooms for the learning impaired taught me how delightful and insightful these students are. I gained an entirely new appreciation for them and the teachers who regularly work in this environment. And the lessons of gentleness and patience I took away from this experience I could apply to my work with other, more gifted students. One size does not fit all; consequently, schools need to be fluid, flexible institutions ready to adapt to individual student learning styles and situations.

Tough Love

I suppose you could say that I have a "tough love" attitude toward education. I have a dream of what it could be, but then those obstacles surface. I love education, so I have to be tough about the maintenance of quality. Staff members who do not have the requisite skills, both professional and personal, have to go. People who don't care about kids and put them first should find another career in which to apply their talents. Administrators who grasp at power and control should not be in our schools. Board members who think in terms of dollars only, or in terms of their own child as opposed to what is best for the school as a whole, might better serve the community in other positions.

The last paragraph was easy to write. The tasks, however, are not easy to do. As a teacher, sometimes I was impatient and undoubtedly hurt some of my students. As an administrator, I have felt threatened by shared governance. I have seen my ideas blocked by colleagues who did not want to change or who literally could not understand the changes I proposed. I did not make a sufficient effort to understand their points of view. I have sat by helplessly as teachers' associations protected the positions of teachers who should not have been in the profession—good people who could have contributed to society elsewhere, but not as teachers. At times, I have failed to listen to others as well as I should have. I have been part of decisions that hurt people.

What I am trying to say is that human beings have extraordinary potential. Hundreds of people can collaborate to send a man to the moon. We can, then, collaborate to bring excellent education to our youth. We can see the world as bigger than ourselves. We can develop education as a profession so that we are treated as professionals. We can be accountable without someone telling us everything to do. Success will be the result of courage, risk, and will, as it should be. After all, we are speaking of the preparation and care of our children.

> Some say that my teaching is nonsense.
> Others call it lofty but impractical.
> But to those who have looked inside themselves,
> this nonsense makes perfect sense.
> And to those who put it into practice,
> this loftiness has roots that go deep. (Lao-tzu, 1988, p. 67)

References

Acheson, K. A., & Gall, M. D. (1987). *Techniques in the clinical supervision of teachers: Preservice and inservice applications.* New York: Longman.

Archer, J. (2002, April 10). Philanthropies seek teacher-training models. *Education Week, 21*(30), 5.

Bambino, D. (2002, March). Critical friends. *Educational Leadership, 59*(6), 25–27.

Blair, J. (2003). With support, teachers would stay put, report finds. *Education Week, 22*, 5.

Brighton, C. M. (1999). Keeping good teachers: Lessons from novices. In M. Scherer (Ed.), *A better beginning: Supporting and mentoring new teachers* (pp. 197–201). Alexandria, VA: Association for Supervision and Curriculum Development.

Brooks, M. (1999). Mentors matter. In M. Scherer (Ed.), *A better beginning: Supporting and mentoring new teachers* (pp. 53–59). Alexandria, VA: Association for Supervision and Curriculum Development.

Carlson, R. V., & Ducharme, E. R. (Eds.). (1987). *School improvement—Theory and practice: A book of readings.* Lanham, MD: University Press of America.

Cavanaugh, S. (2002). Illinois bill stiffens testing rules for aspiring teachers. *Education Week, 21*, 20.

Charkes, A., Cassidy, M., & Olson, N. (2001). *Mentoring and colleague support in Vermont schools 2001.* Brattleboro, VT: Teacher Knowledge Project.

Coppenhaver, A., and Schaper, L. (1999). Mentoring the mentors. In M. Scherer (Ed.), *A better beginning: Supporting and mentoring new teachers* (pp. 60–68). Alexandria, VA: Association for Supervision and Curriculum Development.

Danielson, C. (1996). *Enhancing professional practice: A framework for teaching.* Alexandria, VA: Association for Supervision and Curriculum Development.

Danin, R., & Bacon, M. A. (1999). What teachers like (and don't like) about mandated induction programs. In M. Scherer (Ed.), *A better beginning: Supporting and mentoring new teachers* (pp. 202–209). Alexandria, VA: Association for Supervision and Curriculum Development.

Darling-Hammond, L. (1994). Developing professional development schools: Early lessons, challenge, and promise. In L. Darling-Hammond (Ed.), *Professional Development Schools* (pp. 1–27). New York: Teachers College Press.

Darling-Hammond, L. (2003, May). Keeping good teachers: Why it matters, what leaders can do. *Educational Leadership, 60*(8), 8–13.

DeValle, E., & de Vise, D. (2003). Wanted by fall: 20,000 teachers. MiamiHerald.com. Available: http://nl.newsbank.com/nl-search/we/Archives?p_action=doc&p_docid=0FB51E614BBD75CE&p_docnum=7&s_orderid=NB0103070402145019791&s_dlid=

DL0103070402162019951&s_username=KRDB817872. (Downloaded on June 6, 2003)

Feiman-Nemser, S., Carver, C., Schwille, S., & Yusko, B. (1999). Beyond support: Taking new teachers seriously as learners. In M. Scherer (Ed.), *A better beginning: Supporting and mentoring new teachers* (pp. 3–11). Alexandria, VA: Association for Supervision and Curriculum Development.

Gardner, H., Csikszentmihalyi, M., & Damon, W. (2001). *Good work.* New York: Basic Books.

Glickman, C. D. (1985). *Supervision of instruction: A developmental approach.* Newton, MA: Allyn & Bacon.

Glickman, C. D., Allen, L. R., & Lunsford, B. F. (1994). Voices of principals from democratically transformed schools. In J. Murphy & K. S. Louis (Eds.), *Reshaping the principalship* (pp. 203–218). Thousand Oaks, CA: Corwin.

Goldhammer, R., Anderson, R. H., & Krajewski, R. J. (1980). *Clinical supervision: Special methods for the supervision of teachers.* New York: Holt, Rinehart & Winston.

Goodnough, A. (2002). Klein to announce creation of institute for new principals. *New York Times.* Available: http://query.nytimes.com/gst/abstract.html?res=F5OC12F73FEOC728DDDABO994DA4O4482. (Downloaded April 23, 2003)

Gordon, S. P., & Maxey, S. (2000). *How to help beginning teachers succeed* (2nd ed.). Alexandria, VA: Association for Supervision and Curriculum Development.

Grossman, P. (1994). In pursuit of a dual agenda: Creating a middle level professional development school. In L. Darling-Hammond (Ed.), *Professional development schools* (pp. 50–73). New York: Teachers College Press.

Harvey, J. E., Heller, D. A., McConnell, J. S., & Williams, D. J. (1998). Three new teachers in the English department. In I. Hayes (Ed.), *Great beginnings: Reflections and advice for new English language arts teachers and the people who mentor them* (pp. 139–143). Urbana, IL: National Council of Teachers of English.

Heller, D. (1994). The problem with power. In D. R. Walling (Ed.), *Teachers as leaders: Perspectives on the professional development of teachers* (pp. 287–297). Bloomington, IN: Phi Delta Kappa Educational Foundation.

Heller, D. A. (1989). *Peer supervision: A way of professionalizing teaching.* Bloomington, IN: Phi Delta Kappa Educational Foundation.

Howard, Tyrone C. (2003, Winter). Who receives the short end of the shortage? Implications of the U.S. teacher shortage on urban schools. *Journal of Curriculum and Supervision, 18,* 142–160. Available: http://ascd.org/readingroom/jcs/03winter/howard.html. (Downloaded April 23, 2003)

Hudson, J. S. (2002, March). Friday forums. *Educational Leadership, 59*(6), 76–77.

James, S., Heller, D., & Ellis, W. (1992). Peer assistance in a small district: Windham Southeast, Vermont. In C. D. Glickman (Ed.), *Supervision in transition: 1992 yearbook of the Association for Supervision and Curriculum Development* (pp. 97–112). Alexandria, VA: Association for Supervision and Curriculum Development.

Johnson, S. M., Birkeland, S., Kardos, S. M., Kauffman, D., & Peske, H. G. (2001). Retaining the next generation of teachers: The importance of school-based support. *Harvard Education Letter, 17,* 6–8.

Johnson, S. M., & Kardos, S. M. (2002, March). Keeping new teachers in mind. *Educational Leadership, 59*(6), 12–16.

Kelly, K. (2001, May/June). Teachers helping teachers. *Harvard Education Letter, 17,* 5.

Lambert, L. (1998). *Building leadership capacity in schools.* Alexandria, VA: Association for Supervision and Curriculum Development.

Lao-tzu. (1988). *Tao Te Ching* (Stephen Mitchell, Trans.). New York: HarperCollins.

Levine, M. (2002, March). Why invest in professional development schools? *Educational Leadership, 59*(6), 65–67.

Loucks-Horsley, S., Harding, C., Arbuckle, M., Murray, L., Dubea, C., & Williams, M. (1987). *Continuing to learn: A guidebook for teacher development.* Andover, MA, and Oxford, OH: Regional Laboratory for Educational Improvement of the Northeast and Islands and National Staff Development Council.

Martin, S., & Robbins, K. (1999). Induction: The first five days. In M. Scherer (Ed.), *A better beginning: Supporting and mentoring new teachers* (pp. 27–33). Alexandria, VA: Association for Supervision and Curriculum Development.

Miller, L., & Silvernail, D. L. (1994). Wells junior high school: Evolution of a professional development school. In L. Darling-Hammond (Ed.), *Professional Development Schools* (pp. 28-49). New York: Teachers College Press.

Moffett, C. A. (2000, April). Sustaining change: The answers are blowing in the wind. *Educational Leadership, 57*(7), 35–38.

Moir, E., Gless, J., & Baron, W. (1999). A support program with heart: The Santa Cruz project. In M. Scherer (Ed.), *A better beginning: Supporting and mentoring new teachers* (pp. 106–115). Alexandria, VA: Association for Supervision and Curriculum Development.

Moreno, S. (2003). D.C. schools tapped for principal training. *Washington Post.* Available: http://www.washingtonpost.com/ac2/wp-dyn?pagename=article&node=&contentId=A26767-2003Feb4&notFound=true. (Downloaded April 23, 2003)

Murphy, J., & Louis, K. S. (1994). The evolving role of the principal: Some concluding thoughts. In J. Murphy & K. S. Louis (Eds.), *Reshaping the principalship: Insights from transformational reform efforts* (pp. 265–281). Thousand Oaks, CA: Corwin Press.

National Staff Development Council. (2001). NSDC standards for staff development. Available: http://www.nsdc.org/library/standards2001.html. (Downloaded November 10, 2002)

Oakley, E., & Krug, D. (1991). *Enlightened leadership.* New York: Simon & Schuster.

Patterson, J. L. (1993). *Leadership for tomorrow's schools.* Alexandria, VA: Association for Supervision and Curriculum Development.

Pierce, M. (2000, September/October). Portrait of the "super principal." *Harvard Education Letter, 16,* 6–7.

Renard, L. (1999). Ask not what your school can do for you, but what you can do for you. In M. Scherer (Ed.), *A better beginning: Supporting and mentoring new teachers* (pp. 225–232). Alexandria, VA: Association for Supervision and Curriculum Development.

Rosenblum, S., Louis, K., & Rossmiller, R. (1994). School leadership and teacher quality of work life in restructuring schools. In J. Murphy & K. S. Louis (Eds.), *Reshaping the principalship: Insights from transformational reform efforts* (pp. 99–122). Thousand Oaks, CA: Corwin Press.

Routman, R. (2002, March). Teacher talk. *Educational Leadership, 59*(6), 32–35.

Russo, A. (2002, November/December). Beefing up professional development. *Harvard Education Letter, 18,* 1–3.

Saphier, J. (1993). *How to make supervision and evaluation really work.* Carlisle, MA: Research for Better Teaching.

Scherer, M. (2002, March). Perspectives: Job one. *Educational Leadership, 59*(6), 5.

Schultz, B. (1999). Combining mentoring and assessment in California. In M. Scherer (Ed.), *A better beginning: Supporting and mentoring new teachers* (pp. 99–105). Alexandria, VA: Association for Supervision and Curriculum Development.

Sergiovanni, T. J., & Starratt, R. J. (1971). *Emerging patterns of supervision: Human perspectives*. New York: McGraw-Hill.

Snyder, J. (1994). Perils and potentials: A tale of two professional development schools. In L. Darling-Hammond (Ed.), *Professional development schools* (pp. 98–125). New York: Teachers College Press.

Sparks, D., & Hirsh, S. (1997). *A new vision for staff development*. Alexandria, VA: Association for Supervision and Curriculum Development.

Steinberg, J. (2003). Lessons: One principal's world (the unscripted version). *New York Times*. Available: http://query.nytimes.com/gst/abstract.html?res=FB0D16FF385B0C728CDDA80894DB404482. (Downloaded April 23, 2003)

Stigler, J., and Hiebert, J. (1999). *The Teaching Gap: Best Ideas from the World's Teachers for Improving Education in the Classroom*. New York: Free Press.

Sun Tzu. (2001). *The art of war* (The Denma Translation Group, Trans.). Boston: Shambala.

Viadero, D. (2002, April 10). Researcher skewers explanations behind teacher shortage. *Education Week, 21*(30), 7.

Willis, S. (2002, March). Creating a knowledge base for teaching: A conversation with James Stigler. *Educational Leadership, 59*(6), 6–11.

Wise, A. E. (2003, April 9). What's wrong with teacher certification? *Education Week, 22*(30), 56, 42–43.

Wong, H. (2002, March). Induction: The best form of professional development. *Educational Leadership, 59*(6), 52–54.

Index

Information contained in figures is indicated by an italic *f* following the page number.

About the Author

Daniel A. Heller is the district curriculum coordinator for the Windham Southwest Supervisory Union in Wilmington, Vermont. He has taught secondary English, been a high school English department head, taught graduate-level education courses, served as a director of professional development, and been a principal during his 28-year career in education, both public and private. Heller holds a B.A. in English from Middlebury (Vermont) College, an M.A. in English literature from the Bread Loaf School of English (Vermont), a M.Ed. in curriculum and instruction from Keene (New Hampshire) State College, and a certificate of advanced graduate study from the University of Vermont. Besides the study of literature and writing, his major area of interest is professional development. He has previously published articles and book chapters for *Phi Delta Kappa*, the National Council of Teachers of English, and the Association for Supervision and Curriculum Development.

Heller enjoys reading, writing, developing educational programs, gardening, and fishing. He is particularly fond of long, philosophical discussions, during which he refers to himself as a cynical idealist. He lives in Brattleboro with his wife, Nina, and their dog, Stanley Kowalski. He can be reached at helrdan@sover.net.

Related ASCD Resources

At the time of publication, the following ASCD resources were available; for the most up-to-date information about ASCD resources, go to http://www.ascd.org. ASCD stock numbers are noted in parentheses.

Audiotapes

New Teacher Induction Program: Practical Strategies for New Teachers by Michael La Raus (#200085)

Mentoring: Celebrating and Nurturing the Novice Teacher (#200198)

Networks

Visit the ASCD Web site (http://www.ascd.org) and search for "networks" for information about professional educators who have formed groups around topics such as "Mentoring Leadership and Resources" and "Restructuring Schools." Look in the "Network Directory" for current facilitators' addresses and phone numbers.

Print Products

How to Plan and Implement a Peer Coaching Program by Pam Robbins (#611911)

Keeping Good Teachers edited by Marge Scherer (#104138)

New Teacher Induction: How to Train, Support, and Retain New Teachers by Annette L. Breaux and Harry K. Wong (#303366)

Qualities of Effective Teachers by James H. Stronge (#102007)

Videotapes

Mentoring the New Teacher by James B. Rowly and Patricia M. Hart [series of nine tapes] (#494002)

For more information, visit us on the World Wide Web (http://www.ascd.org), send an e-mail message to member@ascd.org, call the ASCD Service Center (1-800-933-ASCD or 703-578-9600, then press 2), send a fax to 703-575-5400, or write to Information Services, ASCD, 1703 N. Beauregard St., Alexandria, VA 22311-1714 USA.